THE MAGICKAL LANGUAGE

OF THE

BOOK OF THE LAW

an English Qaballa Primer

First published in 2016 by Hadean Press
West Yorkshire
England

WWW.HADEANPRESS.COM

THE MAGICKAL LANGUAGE

OF THE

BOOK OF THE LAW

an English Qaballa Primer

Cath Thompson

For Jim

TABLE OF CONTENTS

FOREWORD

Who am I, to offer a manual of English Qaballa? Please note the spelling, one B, two Ls, as it refers specifically to the system discovered by James Lees in November 1976 and was chosen by him because as he said "no-one else was using that spelling at the time." I am his literary executor, and for over thirty years until Lees' death in 2015 I was his secretary and his archivist, his assistant, his priestess, his companion, and his housekeeper.

When I inherited James Lees' notes and diaries recording his unique pioneering journeys with the English Qaballa I enquired of the remaining members of the O∴A∴A∴ Second Order what they thought I should do with it all. The answer was rapid and unanimous. "Write the book," they said. I suppose it was pretty obvious that I should undertake this task, although it was equally clear to me at least that to do the system justice would need more than one volume. For make no mistake, the English Qaballa is a complete system of Magick both practical and theoretical, with coherent philosophy, stable Mandala, infinite correspondences, and Holy Book.

The present work is not a history of the English Qaballa nor is it a detailed exegesis of English Qaballistic philosophy; it is simply intended as an introduction to the system, a beginner's guide to the Citadel as it were, to which end I have given the ground plan and described the main areas of interest. The basic techniques of E.Qaballistic work are presented also, with a variety of examples which adequately demonstrate the manner in which the English Qaballa picks up the stitches that were dropped centuries ago, untangling the filaments of half-remembered traditions, unpicking the false knots, carding all strands and laying them straight and true for spinning out the warp threads on the loom of the New Aeon. Here you will find how to build the loom for yourself, and begin weaving the fabric of your chosen garment – it is not difficult work for there are relatively few essentials: a copy of *Liber AL* and a calculator; a pure heart and a keen eye for observing Nature; some knowledge of the principles of Astrology, of myth and legend, and of other occult systems; and there should be no damage to existing beliefs beyond the overturning of the odd sacred cow whose characteristics simply cease to make sense, providing only that the student be honest enough to let it fall rather than attempt resuscitation.

And who are you, reading my words? You may wish to find out, and if you come exploring into the Citadel of the English Qaballa you might just discover your True Self peeping out from behind that diadem of the English language that is the *Book of the Law*. Then again, you might be already disenchanted and ready to put this book down – do so, go your way. You have all eternity in which to find the Truth, there's no need to rush.

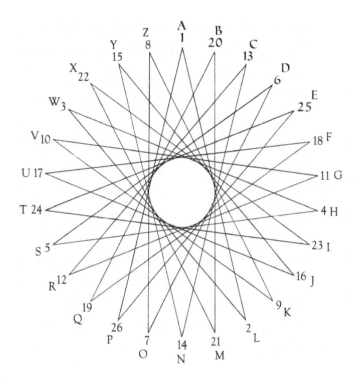

A=1 L=2 W=3 H=4 S=5 D=6 O=7 Z=8 K=9 V=10 G=11
R=12 C=13 N=14 Y=15 J=16 U=17 F=18 Q=19 B=20
M=21 X=22 I=23 T=24 E=25 P=26

I wish to thank Richard, Will, and Davey, for all their support and encouragement of this literary endeavour.

PART ONE

PRELIMINARIES

THE ENGLISH QABALLISTIC methods and guidelines described in the following pages were proposed, tried, and tested by those initiates of the O∴A∴A∴ who devoted themselves to the task of proving the English Qaballa following its discovery by the Chief of the Order, James Lees, on November 26, 1976. In 1980 I became the eighth and youngest initiated member – just in time to help with the last two editions of *The New Equinox: British Journal of Magick* under which title there were five magazines published all together, containing some of the early results of the group's work with the new Qaballa. The present work should serve to amplify some of that material while delineating a framework of rules-of-thumb for working with the English Qaballa.

Now it says in the Comment which accompanies the *Book of the Law*, "All questions of the Law are to be decided only by appeal to my writings, each for himself," so there can be no hard and fast laws of English Qaballa, thus its usefulness depends upon the discrimination and common sense of the individual concerned, and we earnestly recommend the employment of these faculties. Nothing can be dyed in stone, as we say, but decades of experience have shown that there are some processes that are fruitful and may lead on to illumination and others that are barren and a complete waste of time.

The first and most obvious rule is to stay with the English language. Crowley was English, the *Book of the Law* was written almost exclusively in English, and its Qaballa was discovered by an Englishman, and developed in the English Midlands. There is simply no need to wander off into other language systems. The English language has encircled the globe irrevocably since *Liber AL* was written, and that fact alone is indicative of its power in this Aeon. English words should be evaluated with English Qaballistic methods: if an idea works in E.Q. it does not need an explanation by means of translation into other languages; one of the things that makes the English Qaballa attractive to born English-speaking occultists is that it works in their mother-tongue, the language of their thoughts and dreams. (This actually leads to an initiatory process of communication between *Liber AL* and the E.Qaballist to which we will return later.)

It is important to keep within the vocabulary of *Liber AL* for the purpose of analysis by English Qaballa. The Lexicon of the *Book* is the primary source of the English Qaballistic system, and the numerical values thereof are the primary symbols. "Follow the numbers!" was almost a battle cry in those early years of experiment and exploration, because the numbers are pure and their meanings cannot be twisted or altered or fudged. Sometimes it seems almost as if the text requires a certain value to be present, as for example with the unusual spelling of the Name AHATHOOR. The initial letter 'A' brings the value of the Name to 60 which is the value of DEATH. It is no good wishing it were otherwise because the juxtaposition of symbols is too difficult, pretending that the Name is spelled HATHOOR which adds to 59, apparently a much easier number and the value of YONI and THE LAW. Honesty is a prerequisite virtue when working with E.Q.

The Lexicon of *Liber AL* comprises around 1300 single words with values ranging from 1 to 231. Some numbers only have one word of that particular value within the text of *Liber AL*; for example, 150=PRIESTESS, 17=HAWK, 231=CIRCUMFERENCE. These single word values have a purity all of their own because there are no other concepts expressible in one word which compare or parallel, or which oppose or support. Where there is a collection of words of the same value the beginner will find some that stand out with easily recognisable meaning and significance, while others may seem to contradict, and yet other words appear to be utterly disassociated. It may be easiest to begin with the words that strike the most harmonious and loudest chords, and trust that in time they may cause the more obscure subjects to resonate. The numerical value is always the prime archetype and supreme symbol, containing all that we find pertaining thereto. Thus 93 is the paradoxical nature of the Virgin(=93) Mother(=93); and the unforseen divide(=93) caused by a visitation of fate's bad fairy is 93, and 93 is again the enduring puzzle that is Time(=93). These statements will be enlarged upon later on.

It is advisable to apply a rough grading system to one's occult vocabulary when working the English

Qaballistic system, to avoid cluttering up the analysis. At the top of the hierarchy are the words written by Crowley that form the text of the *Book of the Law* and the Lexicon of *Liber AL*, words which shield a significance far greater than any other for the E.Qaballist. The words added to the manuscript by Crowley's wife Rose are of parallel and equal importance. The next rank is held by Names, Titles, and Words that have obvious relevance by virtue of their prominence in current use and their ancient and traditional provenance, such as the names of the Stellar and mythological deities, and the titles of the Tarot Trumps. Also included in this rank are words which are notable by their absence from the text of *Liber AL* such as "cup," "South," and "air." There are many phrases in *Liber AL* mentioning the stars, making it clear that planetary and zodiacal names carry sufficient E.Qaballistic weight to supplement the Lexicon. Nigh on 40 years of study and experimentation support this proposition.

The other Class A material is also of great significance but needs careful assessment and must be used sensibly; the linguistic style is clearly from the same source as *Liber AL* but is more or less obfuscated by the intrusion of the scribe's own consciousness, resulting in at best a close approximation, and parody at the worst. Discrimination is one of the E.Qaballist's most useful weapons when dealing with these documents, where some words are obviously important, and some words equally obviously less so. The other writings by Crowley which have the Class A designation are not the primary texts of the English Qaballistic system and the lexicon of that material must be employed with care by the E.Qaballistic exegetist.

Then there is a panoply of esoteric, occult, and religious phraseology, with many words which may be important to the individual or useful in some particular area of study, but which lack the purity of the symbolism of *Liber AL*; they should be treated as somewhat secondary or perhaps lesser systems. Finally we have the rest of the English language, whose words may be temporarily elevated above their humdrum exoteric status to demonstrate a proposition already made or to amplify a point already sharpened. Discrimination must always be used, and honesty, for it is very much for the individual to decide by intuition and instinct and even divination if necessary whether he or she is on the right track.

To sum up, it is a fundamental premise of the English Qaballa that the Lexicon of *Liber AL* is composed of words of peculiar significance which sets them apart from words which do not appear in *Liber AL*. These words and their numerical values are the core and bedrock of the English Qaballistic system. The individual letters of the English Alphabet too have their own meanings and correspondences – LETTERS=117, which for reasons that will be made clear later on is a number ascribed to the sphere of Kether in manifestation, which is to say the highest level of archetypal symbolism that we may consciously apprehend. The study of the letters is a work not to be put aside by the E.Qaballist.

The fact that we have a Qaballa in English is a piece of compelling evidence for the existence of a Higher Power which we may as well call God and have done. This is a Higher Power which has co-ordinated the development of several languages that predate those of Ancient Greece and Rome – which are tap roots of the European languages, all of which have fed into English – right up to April 1904 when Crowley sat down in his Cairo hotel room and began to take the dictation of the *Book of the Law*. The spellings and grammar of *Liber AL* are the product of millennia, and only God can do that sort of thing – for by what other word may we refer to that which brought the English language into being and nurtured its growth and development over the untold centuries until it blossomed on the pages of Crowley's notebook in the spring of 1904? What other, lesser quality could we ascribe to that which inspired the rules of English grammar and spelling, ordered its alphabet, designed its letters and decreed that they be 26 in number? How else can we think of that which brought about the enumeration of those letters and produced thereby the most comprehensive and far reaching system of correspondences known to Man?

No! *Liber AL* is the work of God. It is a Holy Book: its words and the letters that make up those words have a sanctity of symbolic meaning and therefore must not be altered – the *Book* itself tells us so several times – and moreover, "the original...writing" and "the chance shape of the letters and their position to one another" (*Liber AL* Ch.III v.47), are of such importance that the printed text should always be accompanied by a reproduction of Crowley's handwritten pages; but a disquisition on that material is beyond the scope of the present work and we must leave it there.

I have included the Lexicon of *Liber AL* together with the planetary and zodiacal names, with their numerical values according to English Qaballa at the end of this book.

Part Two

CORRESPONDENCES

A KNOWLEDGE OF correspondences is essential for anyone desirous of engaging in any serious occult work. The magickian who has a comprehensive set of correspondences at his or her disposal can examine any phenomenon and determine its symbolism, which is handy because if you can trace the correspondences of a thing you can judge its reality and if you can do that you can affect its reality. Systems of divination work by correspondences between the material world and the particular units of the system in question, be they Tarot Cards, or I-Ching Hexagrams, or Rune-stones; their function is in their correspondence with the given number of different factors of human experience which they represent. It follows therefore that the scope of the divination is predicated upon the possible combinations of those factors. The accuracy of interpretation depends upon the operator's knowledge and skill in understanding the interactions between the represented archetypal factors and how the story of the question and the answer may be played out according to their peculiar conditions and parameters. The mind of the individual performing the divination ideally works as a library catalogue of the archetypes pertaining to the chosen system, making the combinations of forces and characteristics easy to access and synthesise into an answer comprehensible to the querent. Similarly, the student of the occult will build in his or her mind a catalogue of magickal correspondences which should be capable of accommodating everything in that individual's experience, so that there is nothing that is not incorporated and given its appropriate place.

On a fairly simple level, for instance, reality can be apprehended as being composed of four qualities which correspond to the four elements of Earth, Air, Fire, and Water. These four elements have links with the cardinal points of North, East, South, and West, and each has a weapon assigned to it – thus Earth has a Pantacle or disk, Air has a Knife, the Wand is the weapon of Fire, and to Water is assigned the Cup. The Knife and Wand are interchangeable depending on the particular system being used, but that need not detain us. The point is that there is always a tendency towards either Earthy stability or the free mobility of Air, or Fiery strength, or the gentle nurturing of Water: this is why and wherefore the Lesser Arcana of the Tarot are arranged in four Elemental Suits. Objects are primarily platforms or cutters or pointers or containers, and in ritual it is as well to know these things as they will cause detrimental results later on if used inappropriately. A lot of practical witchcraft is based on this fourfold correspondence, with the addition of the four phases of the Moon and the seasonal Sun cycle; and of course the Hebrew system of correspondences is characterized by the fourfold Name of God, יהוה. The symbol of the Cross is as old and widespread as humanity and all its varied forms resonate the same set of ideas.

They might seem to be dry old traditions of a bygone age, but they are in fact as real and true now as they were a thousand centuries ago, travelling in time from aeon to aeon as perforce they must if they are indeed real and true. That's why we put the Altar in the East of the Temple and enter from the North, and for seasonal rituals stand in the quarters and wear robes coloured according to the Element whose force we wish to contact; the harmonizing by correspondences with what we might call Universal Laws works both ways as the alchemists of old knew well.

Star-based rituals employ the traditional zodiacal and planetary correspondences, which include shape, colour, perfume, weapon, and glyph. For example, suppose you want to invoke Jupiter, whose number incidentally is 4, to bless something with abundance and prosperity. It might be a talisman for good fortune, or a tree planting, or a party, or the inauguration of some undertaking that you hope will expand and lead on to something more and better. For the occasion you would have royal purples and blues in prominent display. You would have incense of cedar. You would have music from the most regal Renaissance court occasions of joy and celebration. You would have things arranged in fours and in squares, and food would be presented as a rich and plentiful banquet with red meat rather than white. All of these conditions are traditional correspondences of Jupiter and if correctly used must inevitably create an environment suitable to be inhabited by a spark of that gloriously majestic force which we call Jupiter. Moreover, if possible, the timing of the event should be synchronised when the beneficent influence of the planet is closely mediated by means of a harmonious aspect with the Moon, for She is our nearest luminary and reflects the rhythms of the Zodiacal Dance most intimately into our lives. Stellar Magick is relatively easy to accomplish with a set of Elemental Weapons and a current ephemeris; and the quaternary arrangement is never far away with the cardinal times of sunrise, midday, sunset and midnight, the division of the heavens into multiples of four, and so on.

The above digression serves to illustrate the practical usefulness of magickal correspondences. The reason for learning them is that one is also learning an orderly arrangement of archetypes which are universal constants visible all the time if one has the eyes to see, and superimposing that arrangement onto the mind. This new structure will then be reinforced by correspondence with observable phenomena and refined by personal experience, which makes life a lot more interesting and fun and generally stops us from going mad – and gives us something coherent to come back to when we do lose our minds. This is useful with reference to the kind of meditational work wherein the student learns to raise the level of consciousness. Knowledge of the correspondences facilitates the continued focussing of the mind by the student; dreams and visionary experiences can be accurately judged and interpreted, and delusion and fantasy more easily avoided.

The English Qaballa forges links of correspondences between a given number and one or more symbols, archetypes, ideas, stories, theories or hypotheses that previously would have been a disassociated jumble.

This gradually rearranges the mind of the E.Qaballist and eventually produces a consistently structured consciousness, capable of extending from the infinitely tiny to the infinitely large in a matrix ranging unequivocally from the creation of the Universe to the dynamics of human relationships. Of course any system of correspondences will do something of the sort, but E.Q. happens to be right up to date and capable of encompassing, harmonizing and incorporating every system of archetypes expressible in English. Numbers cannot lie, or dissimulate, or be anything other than what they are, and if the numbers do not add up then it is we who are wrong.

The correspondences of English Qaballa work through the numeric values of the words in the *Book of the Law*: for example, the word STAR adds up to 42, and so does the word CROSS. This is a correspondence which links in to Christianity where we have the Star of Bethlehem and the Cross of Golgotha. Another correspondence of significance in this context is BLOOD=42. These three words have a correlation which is easy to grasp, and which is coalesced in the numeric symbol 42, from whence the correspondences come reaching out again to other ideas of the cross, or the star, or the blood. To continue with the Christian theme, Jesus, who promises eternal life, has the same value as life. The name JESUS adds to 68 and so does the word LIFE; remember that the number is the primary symbol, and the establishment interpretations of the Biblical testimonies can be set safely on one side. Only LIFE can give life.

When some familiarity with the text of *Liber AL*, its Lexicon, and the E.Qaballistic Alphabet has been acquired, the student will doubtless find his or her interest stimulated by a particular word, phrase, or number, and its correspondences; and will inevitably come up with a calculated result that seems to ring true, or to resonate with some established model. Now if this bit of analysis is going to be of any use it must be synthesised - which is to say, it must find its place in the cosmological microcosm of the student's understanding. Nearly anyone can add numbers together, but there should be a discernible echo as it were in other older systems if there is any truth in the new pattern. Indeed, it sometimes happens that the new pattern has a purity which cuts through the degradation of centuries to reveal the original root idea. Astrology furnishes a set of archetypes through which the Tree of Life may illuminate, or vice versa; then there are other esoteric or mythological or scientific or religious or biological paradigms with which the first set of ideas should resonate. Testing E.Q. against other systems keeps us honest. This assimilation may be harder to accomplish than the calculation, or it may happen in a flash as it were, the pieces joining up so fast we cannot recall where they were before. These 'Eureka' moments may render the student speechless, or helpless with laughter, or flooded with awe.

English Qaballa is an interface between the *Book of the Law* and the English Qaballist, and the *Book of the Law* decoded by the English Qaballa is an initiating force to be reckoned with. The text may seem to be informative but with the application of E.Q. and with the attributions of

E.Q. the effect is not to merely add more data but rather to rearrange the information already present in one's mind into a coherent structure based upon numbers, incorruptible numbers. This is the essence of magickal research, and it involves the removal of barriers existing between the personal and the collective mind so that the individual may perceive the true nature of things. Reason cannot reach beyond the 8th Sephirah, Hod; if the accumulation of information ever got anyone anywhere in the Mysteries then the authors of the Encyclopaedia Britannica should be up there with the gurus. The most that an ordinary book can do is be a map or a signpost: the journey is within yourself, and of course the ultimate book to be read and studied is Nature.

The *Book of the Law* communicates directly with the unconscious (as it is usually called, although 'superconscious' is a term more accurately descriptive of the Higher Mind); the conscious mind just reacts to the apparent meanings of the text, while the text gets on with adjusting the architecture of the psyche. The integration of the mind with the structure of the cosmos as the basis for negotiation through space-time is only the beginning – do not run away because it is uncomfortable, initiation always is. Initiation is attained by superimposing the structure of the cosmic mind upon the individual mind. This always produces conflict with an unbearable desire to do something else – anything else. The surface mind does not object strongly to change but the unconscious mind does and will always test a symbol with resistance. It is the resolution of the resistance that leads to transformation and thus initiation.

The conscious mind has little to do with these negotiations. The *Book of the Law* is a document that initiates more upon every reading; it is the exception to the rule. Reading the *Book of the Law* should set up conflicts and diversions and all kinds of concepts that the psyche must experience as the next step to true enlightenment. Actually it would be more true to say that the *Book of the Law* reads you, working like a computer program in the psyche, its primary function being to align the psyche with the cosmos.

When you first read the *Book of the Law*, if you find that there is no passage within the text that does not appal you then the *Book* is not for you: but if you find there are some parts that do trouble you, then this is the first test and the pointer to the next step, if you have the courage and the humility to take it. Be damned to the concepts that you agree with, you will learn nothing from them, and merely gain a flattered ego for a moment. No! Deal with what you cannot stomach: you know what the concept is, calculate its value and discover what it does by finding its Word, reverse its number and find its Reward, use all your Qaballistic skills upon it and then wait, and slowly but surely the true meaning of this discarded idea will dawn on you.

PART THREE

METHODS

WE WILL NOW discuss the different methods of applying the English Qaballa to the text of *Liber AL vel Legis* which were developed in the late 1970s by members of the O.˙.A.˙.A.˙. under the leadership of Brother Leo (aka James Lees). In describing the various methods of our Qaballa it is important that nothing is given away regarding the initiated mysteries of our Order and yet at the same time the validity of the system is adequately illustrated. In addition it is my purpose to introduce some of the main themes which resonate throughout the *Book*: I am aware that Qaballistic working does not read so easily off the page as it flows through the mind, nonetheless the student should not be daunted, the principal *modus operandi* are quite simple and no doubt correspondences not mentioned here will suggest themselves as the system of the Qaballa begins to infuse itself into the consciousness.

We will commence with an investigation into the nature of Jesus Christ according to the English Qaballa. The name and the qualities commonly attributed to it will be known to most readers, and we have chosen to use it for that reason rather than take a more obscure name or title for our demonstration. A hitherto unknown technique of exploration applied to familiar ground may thus be made clearer and easier to follow.

The *Book of the Law* mentions Jesus once, in Ch.III v.51, with particularly unpleasant imagery guaranteed to dissuade all but the most seriously dedicated student who will understand that one must not look at just the literal meanings in the text. Any impression that since he is only mentioned once Jesus is unimportant to the new Aeon must be discarded, along with any concerns about what we may call establishment Christianity and the many religious forms thereof that have extended from the books of the Old and the New Testament of the Holy Bible. We have no interest in the politics that have been the hallmark of Christianity almost since its inception; we are conducting a completely new examination of the symbol-name JESUS in the completely new light of the English Qaballa. The choice of JESUS as a word to study will not only shed light on the past Aeon but will indicate the continued presence and importance of Jesus in our present Aeon and all aeons to come.

THE FIRST METHOD of Qaballa is simply to calculate the value of a name, phrase, sentence etc, and compare it with others of the same value. The numbers are the primary idea rather than the names or concepts that they resonate. JESUS=68. In the English Qaballistic system 6=LAW and 8=0 or infinity. This is based on *Liber AL* Ch.I v.46, "Nothing is a secret key of this law...I call it eight..." and that the symbol for infinity is an 8 on its side. Therefore we may say that 68 is Law expressed to Infinity or Infinite Law, and Jesus is a resonance or expression of this Law.

JESUS = 68 = LIFE, CHANGE. It is certainly true that the infinite law is LIFE and CHANGE. Everything that lives, changes; this is not merely a statement of physical evolution, for life is not necessarily bound into form. The infinite law of life is change; everything lives, and nothing that lives remains the same. The symbol of JESUS illustrates to the Initiate how life and change proceed through time. In the change from one form of energy to the next it is necessary that some of the original energy is given up. Jesus led a life of sacrifice, simply illustrating that to move forward in time something must be sacrificed.

Change is the formula of Life but its mechanisms are not uniform or indeed logical, proceeding according to the 93 formula of unity by denial or division by affirmation. This means that what seems impossible logically must exist by necessity. A bird has feathers exactly because it should not. It is impossible that an evolutionary system could sustain such an event as giving a creature feathers, but for the infinite variety and joy of life it is necessary that it be so. The number 93 and its Magickal Formula will be examined in detail later on; here it will be sufficient to note that 93 is the value of NATURE and TIME, in which all things exist, yet both Nature and Time remain untouched and inviolable.

A SECOND METHOD of our Qaballa is one in which the values of the first letters of each word in a phrase or sentence are added together. The analysis of the resulting number will reveal how the process indicated by the sentence will begin, just as adding the last letters of each word of a sentence will produce a number that describes how the expression will end. The words of the phrase or sentence in question express what will occur between the beginning and the end. To remain within our guidelines we must find a sentence whose initials add to 68. "This shall regenerate the world," (*Liber AL* Ch.1 v.53) is a phrase which meets this requirement. Here the initial letters T+S+R+T+W = 24+5+12+24+3 = 68. The beginning of the regeneration of the world will be with JESUS/LIFE/CHANGE=68. This rejuvenation will be finalised by the sum of the last letters of each word, which is S+L+E+E+D = 5+2+25+25+6 = 63 = VIRGO the Sign of the Virgin. The regeneration of the world will be completed by the Virgin Mother of Jesus, who in her deepest mystical sense is the great Goddess Nuit.

To further illustrate this method consider the phrase in *Liber AL* Ch.II v.15, "For I am perfect," where again 68 is the sum of the initial letters F I A P. Jesus begins the cycle of perfection. How will this perfection end and what will it evolve into? Again we use the last letters of the phrase, R I M T = 80. Now *Liber AL* says in Ch. 1 v. 46 that Nothing is called Eighty, and so for the E.Qaballist the number 80 is a form of Nothing which has the quality of Infinity. We then have the principle of a Perfection which begins with Infinite Law, 68, JESUS, and finishes with Infinite Nothing. This is an affirmation of the formula of creation, the formula of how an idea must ultimately obsess a medium, the basis upon which the magic of manifestation works. Using this method of Qaballa one can divine many of the secrets of the mysteries.

A THIRD METHOD of Qaballa involves reversing the number to find what E.Qaballists call the reward of that number. This method is revealed in the first verse of the third Chapter, "Abrahadabra! The reward of Ra Hoor Khut," where ABRAHADABRA = 79, and 97 = RA HOOR KHUT. The Name (or Title) Ra Hoor Khut, has the E.Qaballistic value 97 and that which this entity bestows – its reward – is Abrahadabra whose value is the same digits reversed, 79. The reward of JESUS = 68 is then 86 which is the E.Qaballistic value of MERCY. We see with this analysis of the symbol-name Jesus that in the philosophy of the English Qaballa he is not in the least judgmental, and his reward is always clemency and compassionate MERCY. 86 is also the value of THE SEAL "of the promise of our agelong love," (*Liber AL* Ch.II v.66).

"COUNTING WELL" is another method derived from the third chapter, involving two words. The value of the first word is multiplied by the number of letters in the second word, and the value of the second word multiplied by the number of letters in the first, and the two totals then added together. JESUS=68 CHRIST=81 and so the calculation is as follows: 68 x 6 = 408, and 81 x 5 = 405, the subtotals giving the sum 408 + 405 = 813. This is the sum total of all the planets by E.Q., which shows that all the planetary influences are harmonised by the power of Jesus Christ:

SUN=36
MOON=49
MERCURY=115
VENUS=71

MARS=39
JUPITER=143
SATURN=73
URANUS=66
NEPTUNE=145
PLUTO=76

Sum total = 813; if we subtract 36=SUN from 813 we find that the numerical value of all the planets without the Sun is 777 – the three faces of the Goddess. It is worth noting that in the Hebrew system 813 is the value of the word ARARITA which means God is one, and the three in one; while in the numerical system of the English Qaballa 813 means the Infinite (8) is one (1) in three forms (3). A divergence between the two systems is that in the Hebrew the supreme deity was male, and *Liber AL* says she is a woman – quite simply, WOMAN=46=ONE.

The method of "counting well" was described at length in TNE/BJM Vol.5 Pt.1, and some time later Jake Stratton-Kent introduced the convention of the % sign as an abbreviation, the symbol being inserted between the pair of words under discussion. Counting well was discovered by Stefan Dajnowicz (Brother Thoth O∴A∴A∴ retired) in the course of a study of the words in *Liber AL* Ch.III v.19 in conjunction with the 19th verses of the first and second Chapters: "That stele they shall call the abomination of desolation; count well its name & it shall be to you as 718,"(*Liber AL* III:19) "O azure-lidded woman, bend upon them,"(*Liber AL* II:19) "...but the highest are of us,"(*Liber AL* I:19). REVEALING has the same value as I AM NUIT, identifying the Stele of

Revealing with the Goddess NUIT = 78. The inclusion of the number 1 means that 718 is a numeric symbol of an archetype of WOMAN = ONE = 1, and we take her to be the "azure-lidded woman" while the "abomination of desolation" refers to Space. The highest phenomenon is always the sky, or space, the Goddess Nuit, the Woman called AZURE-LIDDED = 131 = UNIVERSE. Multiply the value of the first word by the number of letters in the second word (AZURE=63 x6 =378) and multiply the value of the second word by the number of letters in the first word (LIDDED=68 x5 = 340) and then add the two results to count well the Name: 378 + 340 = 718.

IN THE ENGLISH QABALLISTIC SYSTEM the Word or expression of an archetype may be found by adding 34 to its value. This method was derived from *Liber AL* Ch.I v.39 "The word of the Law is Θελημα." This Greek word meaning 'will' in the sense of Divine Will has the value 93 in the Greek system. The number which brings the value of THE LAW (=59) up to 93 is 34: therefore the word of the law is 59 + 34 = 93 = Θελημα. The Word of Jesus is 68 + 34 = 102 = BEAUTY, KNOWLEDGE, THE CROWN, THE KEY. This method is a great source of understanding through contemplative meditation, wherein ideas are gently encouraged to reveal their mysteries by their correspondences. JESUS himself is the Word of SHE=34.

ANOTHER METHOD of English Qaballa involves the spelling of words. The letters of the alphabet each have an individual meaning; when these meanings combined and expressed in a word are examined sequentially, the true meaning of the word is revealed.

J = 16 = WAR;
JE = 41 = HER;
JES = 46 = WOMAN;
JESU = 63 = VIRGO;
JESUS = 68.

WAR is the breakdown and destruction of an earlier status quo as a result of the balancing of forces as indicated by the harmonious number 6 = LAW. This is reiterated in the number 41 where the 4 is a stable fourfold perfection and the 1 is unity; and repeated again with 46 = ONE = WOMAN, and the archetypal perfection of the female is further emphasised with VIRGO the Sign of the Virgin. By analysis using English Qaballa as the primary tool we see that the true meaning of the word JESUS, by which we mean the essential nature of the entity called Jesus, is that of his Mother. He is a God whose power is feminine – he gives love, and healing, and he sustains and nurtures, he is all-embracing, and all-forgiving.

A DERIVATIVE METHOD takes words which appear within words; for example the last two letters of Jesus spell the word US = 22 = X the sign of the Cross. JES =46 = SORROW, Jesus is therefore the Sorrow of the Cross. This method comes from the study of the word 'beast'. THE BEAST = 128 = BAPHOMET. The word splits into BE AS T where T = GOD, and so to assume the Title of Baphomet one must Be As God. Note that AS = 6 = LAW.

To find out the nature of what unites and divides two ideas, simply subtract the smaller value from the greater. Jesus is said to be the Son of God: GOD = 24 and JESUS = 68 are connected or separated by the difference between the two numbers which is 68-24=44 = LOVE: so JESUS is GODLOVE, or the Love of God which is God; and also meaning that Jesus is the God of Love. MAN = 36, therefore that which is between man and Jesus is 68 – 36 = 32 = DOOR, and indeed we must knock if we would enter. 32 is 23 reversed; 23 = I, indicating that the self's identity must be turned on its head, which is in accordance with Christian mystical tradition.

FINALLY, THE CONTEXT OF A WORD sheds light on the meaning of that word. The only place that Jesus is mentioned in *Liber AL* is in Ch. III v.51, "I peck at the eyes of Jesus as he hangs upon the cross." Note that the present tense of the word 'HANGS' means that he still hangs on the cross. This is quite precise, Jesus hangs on the cross throughout all eternity, as Spirit is forever crucified upon the Cross of Matter. The speaker is identified with Horus of the Hawk's head, and since the word PECK has the same value as POWER the phrase can be read "I power (at) the eyes of Jesus," meaning that Horus is a factor of resistance against the eyes of Jesus. Of course at the same time this is the very impediment that causes the phenomenon of those eyes to exist, for it is only by resistance (what Dion Fortune described as "the thrusting block of the engine"), that any phenomenon can occur, and without it all energy will just pass on through until it does find something to react against. To find out about the energy that is in the eyes of Jesus we calculate the E.Qaballistic value of THE EYES OF JESUS. 53+70+25+68 = 216 which is the value of VENUS + NEPTUNE. Neptune is the Astrological god and planet of Mysticism, Venus the Goddess of Love, and so it is the combined influence of these two celestial deities, a divine mystical love synonymous with the Eyes of Jesus that is resisted by Horus and given power thereby. In terms of the English Qaballa, HORUS = 45 is the equivalent of I AM = 45, which is to say that Horus is the ego: all action and energy and positive determination. The avenging Horus, crimson in his glory, is the natural enemy of the gently loving mystic who views everything through the Eyes of Jesus. There is no grace or guilt implicit in this statement, it is a simple fact and an illustration of one of the laws of nature.

IN THE LIGHT OF THESE NEW CORRESPONDENCES we may now embark on an investigation of the nature of CHRIST = 81 = HIDING, STELE, TRUTH, APPEAL, GIVER, KNOWING.

81 in E.Qaballistic terms means Infinite (8) Woman (1 = ONE = WOMAN). The Christ (or the Anointed) has the nature of Infinite Woman, the Goddess. It is important to understand that all the deities are both male and female, bisexual and hermaphroditic: in themselves they are all feminine and receive worship and adoration, and in action they are all masculine, distributing the blessings which are in their nature to bestow. Christ's blessings are of KNOWING(=81) TRUTH(=81). He is the GIVER(=81) to whom anyone may APPEAL(=81).

The second Chapter of *Liber AL* begins "Nu! The hiding of Hadit," which can be read as "Nu! The Christ (Truth, or Knowing) of Hadit." Nu conceals Hadit with TRUTH, the HIDING which is CHRIST. Hadit is the infinitely tiny particle and is in a state of perfect balance as demonstrated by HADIT = LIBRA the Zodiacal Sign of Balance, but this perfect balance must be concealed for manifestation to occur. If the Balance of Hadit were not kept in HIDING then manifestation would swiftly become perfect and cease to exist. In KNOWING this we know TRUTH, in the IMAGE(=81) of CHRIST. CHRIST = 81 = STELE, but *Liber AL* Ch. III v.10 states "The stele of revealing <u>itself</u>," or, the Christ of revealing itself which means that Christ is the formula of revealing ITSELF. In the English Qaballa the word IT refers to the ego of a God, the first letter 'I' being the ego, and T = 24 = GOD. The word 'self' means personal ego, and so ITSELF is the personalised ego of a god. Therefore Christ is the formula whereby the personal ego of a god is to be revealed. The Christ or "stele of revealing itself" is the star that reveals the nature of itself, or unveils the personal ego of a god. The supreme self of IT, the supreme self ITSELF, is revealed by the Stele. That phenomenon that reveals the perfection of all THINGS(=81) is the hidden Christ.

Finally let us find out what separates Man from Christ, which is the way in which Man should aspire to Christ. To do this we simply subtract the one from the other, 81 – 36 = 45 = NOT. In accordance with mystical tradition, the system of the English Qaballa demands that the Aspirant depolarises himself, becoming consciously negative (NOT) to the power called the

Divine Bridegroom. 45 is also the value of HORUS. Man must experience and become Horus before he can be of Christ. HORUS = 45 = I AM. Man must develop for himself a discreet identity peculiar to himself to become Christ. He must be able to say 'I am unchangeable and thus a God'. The way he does this is to follow all the ways of Love through Christ: "there is no bond that can unite the divided but love," (*Liber AL* Ch.I v.41).

Many more words could be written on the subject of the Name of JESUS (and the Title of CHRIST) analysed using the English Qaballa, but I have amply described the nature and characteristics of this particular deity according to the *Book of the Law*. The power of Jesus in the English Qaballistic system is maternal and preserving, and although he himself is male he personifies and demonstrates all the feminine values, for the body from which he issues is female. It is worth remarking that the Word of Christ , 81 + 34 = 115 = MERCURY, resumes the male-female symbolism. It is his female unconscious that drives the conscious male just as it is Venus or the Holy Ghost that is the power behind Christ.

Now I am going to give some more examples of working with the E.Q. using the methods detailed above to examine some other important words. I will keep the correspondences to a minimum so that the student will be able to make his or her own analysis and synthesis. The most precise and accurate description of a mountain top can never approach the experience of going there and seeing it for oneself. I am merely putting up signposts, so that the student may construct a personal map and ascend the peak for himself or herself.

Words, phrases, and sentences of the same value pertain to the same root number archetype. UNIVERSE=131=SUPREME, and SERPENT, and O PROPHET. The Universe is supreme; and it has always been symbolised as a serpent; and the ultimate prophet of O or Nothing could only be everything, which in other words is the Universe. 131 in the Greek Qaballa is the value of PAN, a word which is used in English as a prefix meaning "All".

THE INITIALS OF WORDS that form a series such as a sentence reveal the first phase of the essential nature of the statement. The last letters of the same words similarly reveal the final phase. They give the empirical meaning of the words. For example, the phrase in *Liber AL* Ch.III v.36 "Then said the prophet unto the God" has a total value of 418. This number resonates throughout the Book; here a brief explanation will suffice: 41 is the value of WHOLE, and 8 signifies Infinity, therefore 418 may be said to symbolise the Whole of Infinity. The Universe is the first manifestation of that infinite wholeness; so it is hardly suprising that the initials of the phrase, TSTPUTG=131=UNIVERSE. The sum of the last letters of the words in question, NDETOED, is 107 which is the value of MATTER, the ultimate crystallization of the whole of Infinity. The first and last letters give a root meaning to that which is expressed in the phrase.

An insight into the interplay between archetypes may be gained by subtracting the value of one from that of another. NUIT=78 without HAD=11 is 67, the value of FLAME. Nuit is FIRE (=78); this means that Had is that which is burned by the flame to give the fire of Nuit. The difference between MAN=36 and GOD=24 is 12: Man has within him the twelve signs of the Zodiac, and God does not, having transcended the Zodiac. This is an alternative way of analysing this subtraction of one value from another.

WORDS HAVING A DOUBLE-DIGIT VALUE are their own reward, for example LOVE = 44, CIRCLE = 88. The reward of the Great Goddess Nuit is Her value, 78, reversed which is 87, the value of EIGHT, and GREEN, and MONTHLY. The Goddess gives the greenness of nature; this implies that the complementary colour red is attributable to Her as in "The five-pointed Star with a circle in the middle, & the circle is red," (*Liber AL* Ch.1 v.60). MONTHLY suggests the menstrual flux, a concept further underlined by the representation of the Goddess on Earth that is the Scarlet Woman. BURNT=87 is rather obvious as the reward of FIRE=78.

The reward of THE STAR (=95) is 59, the value of YONI and WHEEL. The symbol of THE STAR is found in all three sections of the Complete Tree of Life, the solution to *Liber AL* Ch. II v.76, pouring the blessings of Heaven from the Top of the Tree onto the roots. (See diagram on page 73.) The Yoni is the reward she gives to her worshippers, the Wheel of Life and its true meaning. There is a great mystery in this, which is beyond the scope of the present work as it contains a very powerful magical formula.

The reward of 93 is 39=MARS and AUM, the

source of all energy in creation, and YOU, for you are also the bearer of all the energy in creation on a microcosmic scale. In the lower worlds Mars tends towards destruction, as indeed does SCORPIO (=93). It is unwise to begin anything when the Moon is in the House of Death, for it will destroy the event; however, magical work, particularly with *Liber AL*, can be unusually productive at this time, due to a link through the planes caused by TAHUTI (=93).

THE WORD OF A DEITY is its value + 34. The word of LOVE is 44 + 34 = 78 = NUIT the Goddess of the Stars, who is divided for love's sake. 78 is also the value of FIRE, cognate with the active principle or force of Love. Crowley said that Abrahadabra was the word of the Aeon – but according to English Qaballa ABRAHADABRA(=79) is the word of HORUS(=45). 79 – 34 = 45. It is inadvisable to utter the word Abrahadabra except during the Supreme Ritual: it is the Word of the END=45 and the "Ending(=93) of the words," (*Liber AL* Ch.III v.75) and tends to provoke destructive results. The word of THE AEON is 53 + 47 + 34 = 134 = DELIVERED, INSPIRED, and UNATTACKED. The word is what the entity or archetype will teach you; the reward is what it will give you.

I HAVE SAID that the significance of a word is dependent upon the values of each letter in its construction for its inner meaning. The result of applying this method is that the word usually means exactly what you think it means in English but this is emphasised in a curious way. For example, the word God is composed of GO=18 and D=6. 6 is the value of LAW, and 18 signifies one to infinity in action or GOing; thus the word Go-D really means the infinite activity of the Law, or, more simply, Law in Action. This method of synthesising the attributes of a word is demonstrated below, using the words HADIT and NUIT.

H=4: the elements, Tetragrammaton, etc.

HA=5: S, the root of the energy of matter, the wave-form, the smallest particle of matter.

HAD=11: two negatively polarized forces; HA=5, D=6, and thus we have the Law of the Pentagram.

HADI=34: the value of LEO and FOOL; energy, the will to be.

HADIT=58: the value of LIBRA, the balance.

HADIT is the root of matter, having as its essential nature the law of the pentagram, and its substance partaking of the Fool and Leo: the balanced but implacable Will to Be of the God-identity of HAD.

N=14: the root letter of Death ('Nun' in Hebrew, ascribed to the Death Tarot Trump).

NU=31: the value of SOUL and WORK; the activity of the wave-form.

NUI=54: the value of SNAKE, embodiment of the wave-form.

NUIT=78: the value of FIRE; the Goddess Infinite, the divine ego of NU.

This is a most apt description of division for love's sake: NUI=54=SNAKE plus T=24=GOD. Nuit manifests in man as the love of God; this is "my name" known to man mentioned in *Liber AL* Ch.I v.22.

To FINISH THIS EXPOSITION of the methods of English Qaballa I will briefly examine a few significant words that do not appear in *Liber AL*. The name Babalon is traditionally interpreted as "The Woman clothed with the Sun" but what does the name mean in E.Q.?

B=20: the root number of MANIFESTATION = 200.

BA=21=M: the initial of Mary Magdalene, etc.

BAB=41=WHOLE, HER: this is complete femininity.

BABA=42=STAR, BLOOD, CROSS, KISS: the mysteries of female physiology.

BABAL=44=LOVE, FOLLY: attributes of her worship.

BABALO=51=ONES: ONE (or WOMAN) with the attributes of S=5, pure energy, the traditional number of Mars.

BABALON=65:=WATER, WINE, WISDOM.

In E.Q. She is the Woman of the Star whose nature is to manifest the power of the supreme Goddess. She is complete, She is the wisdom and the strength and the courage of woman, She is Babalon and quite insatiable. This interpretation is somewhat more comprehensive than the usual and may be extended.

BAPHOMET is another entity of whose nature much has been written but little understood.

B=20: root of manifestation.

BA=21=M: of the nature of the great M.

BAP=47=EGG, GLORY, STARS: life before birth.

BAPH=51=ADORE, ISLAND, ONES: individuality divided.

BAPHO=58=HADIT, LIBRA, HOUSE: the infinitely tiny particle in dynamic balance.

BAPHOM=79=ABRAHADABRA: the Word of Creation.

BAPHOME=104=SECRET, WONDERFUL, HOOR PA KRAAT: the Silent One.

BAPHOMET is the Egg in perfect balance, the secret whose nature is 79. The Egg can contain anything: it is a symbol of life in the making, the mystery. Baphomet is depicted with all the attributes of nature. The Egg has all the attributes of nature, it is Life in potential, ready to be born and is at once secret and apart as the divine will to go.

Finally, MAGICK is a much used word that nobody, I suspect, knows the real meaning of:

M=21: the Goddess in her three forms 3x7=21.

MA=22=X: the ordeal of AL.

MAG=33=SWORD: the weapon of analysis.

MAGI=56=ISIS, RULE: the word of X which is Nuit-in-action.

MAGIC=69=DANGER, GLADNESS: there is success.

MAGICK=78=NUIT.

The art of magick then is a dangerous undertaking involving the winning of the ordeal X, the Ordeal of the Cross: it may be symbolised by the figure of the Woman girt with a Sword who is the Goddess-Queen of Magickal endeavour.

THE BOOK OF THE LAW is full of traps and pitfalls for the unwary reader. It must not only be read merely as one would read any text: every letter of every word has its own meaning, and every word of every phrase has its own significance, and every phrase of every sentence has its own numeric correspondences. *Liber AL* is multi-layered and multi-faceted far beyond the poetic imagery of language with which it veils itself. Verbal quotation from *Liber AL* can be dangerous, as the Comment indicates, "Those who discuss the contents of this Book are to be shunned by all, as centres of pestilence." This is not a ban on dialectics per se, but the words and phrases in *Liber AL* cannot be taken at face value alone, and as the E.Qaballist learns the music of the English Qaballa and begins to play his or her own variations, the Work will become more personal and there will be an almost instinctive antipathy to discussion of results except in allegorical or metaphorical terms; this wisdom may have to be learned in the same way as we learn about fire, and there will almost certainly be some burned fingers along the way.

In the English Qaballa the number is the primary symbol, consequently the Qaballistic interpretation of a phrase or sentence is always derived firstly from the numerical values concerned, and then from their correspondences. The meanings and implications of words are considered in the light of their numbers to begin with, and then the context and the literal, symbolic, metaphorical, scientific, philosophical and magickal meanings are allowed to weave themselves in to the portrait of the archetype which is the particular number in question.

In the groups of words of a given value the student will usually find one or two in the Lexicon of Liber AL which stand out; it may be a Name, or a recognisable force or element, or a concept which is universal: for example, 78 = NUIT and FIRE, and so to the E.Qaballist 78 is fundamentally the symbol of the Goddess Nuit, a primary characteristic of whom is the Element of Fire. 36 = MAN and SUN, and so again the number 36 is the male Solar principle as far as English Qaballa is concerned, and word-symbols such as MASK=36 and HEAD=36 will then be seen to magnify and uphold the numeric symbol. In this fashion the numbers become complex structures of ideas, and if they defy logic and outrage reason so much the better. "Reason is a lie" Liber AL tells us in Ch.II v.32, and occult research has very little to do with logic.

A=1 by E.Q. and the number ONE adds up to 46 which is the value of WOMAN. This means that in the E.Qaballistic philosophy the number one, 1, is the number and symbol of Woman - by which we mean the archetypal Woman who is the manifestation of the Goddess and who inhabits every human female - so that all ideas pertaining to the first digit following zero, also (and more importantly) pertain to Her. This is an extremely significant statement for a magickal alphanumeric system to make, for it brings everything back to the Goddess and says that she is responsible for the Creation.

The numbers back up this assertion with the simple fact that CREATION=EMPRESS by E.Q. There can be no argument; it is well known that all works of creativity partake of the nature of their creator, who can do no more than express what he or she essentially is. Creation stories all start out with a negative feminine principle which we may call the Goddess (although it should be understood that the phenomenon of which we speak is beyond the words of human thought) who, according to *Liber AL*, divided for love's sake into Nothing and less than nothing, which again for love's sake and the chance of union became Something. The process of creation is therefore utterly feminine, with no male intervention. This is reflected in the myths of the Virgin Birth, where the Holy Ghost is traditionally held to be female and sometimes even identified with Venus. Woman, because of her negative polarity, is capable of creation, as well as reproduction.

It is worth remarking that the sex chromosomes in human embryonic cells start out as a female pair and only later is the transformation that brings forth a male child. All numbers are made from 1 as surely as we were born of woman. *Liber AL* is simply reminding us of a fundamental truth which is so obvious and all-pervading as to be easily overlooked. In this fashion the English Qaballa brushes the cobwebs of familiarity from the windows of many a room in the Temple of the E.Qaballist's soul.

It is a theme insisted upon again and again in *Liber AL* that the Supreme First Deity is Female in principle, and Male in action. For example, every use of the word 'me' in *Liber AL* refers to Woman, since ME=46: and each time the word 'my' appears it signifies Man, as MY=36=MAN. With this bit of E.Q. in mind when we read a phrase such as "Help me, o warrior lord of Thebes, in my unveiling before the children of men!" (*Liber AL* Ch. I v.5) we experience an overlapping of ideas around these two numbers, 46=ME and WOMAN and 36=MY and MAN, and achieve thereby a parallel and symbolic understanding of the words which is "help [woman] o warrior lord of Thebes, in [man] unveiling before the children of men." This is a rather fluidic and intuitive technique of reading the enumerated text of the *Book of the Law* which becomes much easier with a little practice. The injunction describes the positive activity of Man and the receptive desire of Woman's negativity.

The system revealed by the E.Q. teaches us the mysteries of the Divine Woman which history has kept hidden and forbidden. Woman is the great initiator, the giver of THE LAW=59=YONI. In the first words of *Liber AL*, "Had! the manifestation of Nuit," the letters H A D have the values 4 1 6, symbolising the snake (SNAKE=54=FOUR), the woman (WOMAN=46=ONE), and the law (D=6=LAW). This accurately describes the Garden of Eden scenario where Eve taught Adam the knowledge of THE SNAKE=107. This number is significant as the value of SUN+VENUS as these two celestial bodies form a pentagram with the points of their conjunctions in the heavens. The shape of the pentagram is found in at the centre of the apple when it is bisected at right angles to the core: the fruit is therefore a symbol of the initiation which Eve bestowed upon Adam. WOMAN=46=SORROW, which is a source of much misunderstanding because it is so true.

In the philosophy of E.Q. and its application to the *Book of the Law* WOMAN=ONE=46, and so all occurrences of the numbers 1 and 46 within the enumerated text of *Liber AL* constitute a reference to Woman. Two digit numbers where the first number is 1 signify a Woman who is expressing the second number, manifesting the power of the subsequent number from within herself, while in the converse case it is a Woman with the nature of the first number, or of that force acting through her.

91 thus refers to the illusion with which the Woman conceals her true nature, 9 being the number of Illusion. A woman is positive on the unconscious level and negative on the conscious level – she has no sense of 'self' in the way that a man, consciously positive, has a central 'self'. HERSELF=91. This Woman of Illusion creates the false representation of the eternal fresh beauty of SPRING(=91) reflected in the feminine desire for eternally youthful beauty. She may APPEAR(=91) and still remain VEILED(=91). Yet this glamourous female by giving an illusory image of herself may provoke dishonesty and therefore be FORSAKEN(=91) and even be seen as an OUTCAST(=91). She is a most

familiar facet of the Goddess and no doubt will be easily recognised.

The number 8 in E.Qaballistic terms is synonymous with Infinity of Nothing as stated in *Liber AL* Ch.I v.46, "Nothing is a secret key....I call it eight, eighty, four hundred and eighteen" since 8 has the same shape as the symbol for Infinity. 81 therefore symbolises the infinite negativity of the eternal Woman, She who is the TRUTH(=81) concealed within the STELE(=81) of Revealing. THE WORD has this value; the Woman of Infinite Nothingness is the Word that is Truth – the most negative aspect of the Goddess has the greatest integrity – 81 is the archetype of an honourable woman but her great negativity makes her difficult to pin down and she is constantly HIDING=81. IMAGE=81 and in Ch.III v.21 it is written, "Set up my image in the east." where MY has the same value as SUN and MAN, 36. The phrase refers to the ultimate and transcendent ideal image of Woman that can be expressed by man, the most beautiful and illuminating Woman Clothed with the Sun. MY IMAGE has the value 117, a number that will be explained later on in the context of the Complete Tree of Life, 117 being the value of Kether on the Tree of Manifestation.

In accordance with tradition from time immemorial, 7 in E.Q. is the number of the Goddess, and 71 is the value and number of VENUS, the Great Goddess expressed in Woman; whose planet bestows all the qualities of beauty; whose love is eternal. 71 is a Woman who inspires love and adoration, and even worship, in all who come into contact with her. Great works of art and poetry, and great deeds of heroism too, are enacted in Her Name. HEARTS has the value 71: all hearts express love, regardless of how the individual names his passion, for the man who hates violence loves peace, and he who loves justice abhors injustice; this is why both love and hate cause the same warm glow in the heart. It is wise to understand this when looking at words such as 'hate' in *Liber AL*.

61 signifies the Woman who embodies the LAW=6 which as *Liber AL* tells us is Love. This Woman's nature is the universal Law of Love. LAW=6, the number symbolising the erect Kundalini serpent united with its source in heaven. She is the expression of the division for love's sake, the secret and most sacred NAME(=61) whose SHAPE is ARCHED to HONOUR the CARESS of creation. As *Liber AL* says, 61 in the Hebrew system is the value of AIN or Nothing, the "secret Key of this law," (Ch.I v.46); it is this law of reunion, through love, of the divided unity, which is at the centre of the Creation as it is both revealed and concealed in the *Book of the Law* and the Completed Tree of Life. The Woman symbolised by 61 is an Initiated Priestess of the Secret Key, for she has balanced the duality of her own nature.

With the number 51 we meet the Woman of the pentagram. The shape of the number 5 indicates the snake; THE SNAKE = 107 = SUN+VENUS and as we know, the pentagram is drawn in the heavens once every eight years by the conjunctions of the Sun and Venus. The Woman of the Star and the Snake is she who has the task of adjusting and purifying humanity, for she is the Kundalini Serpent who ascends the body of man to unite with herself in the highest Chakra. She can be described as that continuous state of change which is the Universe; her action is similar to Karma. 51 is the value of SORROWS, which she appears to provoke and sustain, to those who resist the adjustment that she demands. Her force is practically unstoppable.

The next Woman to consider is signified by the number 41, she who expresses all phenomena dependent on the number 4; the elements, quarters, seasons, and so on. The number four gives us the continuous cycle of birth, life, death, and afterlife. The cycle of eternal life is that of the Woman who is symbolised by the number 41. She is also the third in the triad of ladies whose power comes from the Kundalini Serpent, for FOUR=54=SNAKE; in this case the emphasis is on stability and continuity and therefore the correspondence has more to do with the Snake holding its tail in its mouth.

31 is the value of NU. The Woman of Nu is the SOUL(=31) that conceals the Trinity of Heaven. The second Chapter of *Liber AL* begins with the statement "Nu! the hiding of Hadit." Hadit is the infinitely tiny particle which cannot be seen; it is smaller than any wave-form known to physics. A wave-form must always be used to view another wave-form, or interference in space, such as matter, light, and so on. Physics has shown that upon manifestation a particle explores space and time both backwards and forwards, an event symbolised by the number 58=HADIT, for 5=S the archetypal wave-form of the Snake, in infinity as expressed by the number 8. It is said in Ch.II v.4 that "she shall be known and I never." Wave-forms are known – but

the ultimate disturbance in space that is responsible for manifestation can never be known, in the Gnostic sense. Nu is the wave-form which conceals Hadit, as is signified by the shape of the letters: ⌐⌐⌐

With the number 2 we come to the Woman symbolised by 21. The word TWO=34, the same value as LEO and SHE. This number refers to the Woman leading the Lion illustrated by the Tarot card Strength. Tradition has it that this card represents Mary Magdalene and the Lion of Judea. 21 is the value of the letter M in E.Q. – a letter of great significance to occult lodges as the initial of the Magdalene; and vital in the symbol of the first creation as it is delineated in *Liber AL*. 21 is also the sum of 3x7, all three faces of the Goddess.

The first word of *Liber AL*, HAD, has the value 11, signifying the dual Goddess in the division for love's sake. The essential meaning of the first words of the *Book of the Law*, "Had! the manifestation of Nuit," is equivalent to the Biblical expression of the moment of creation, "Let there be light!" The duality is that of Kether, deity beholding deity as in a mirror. ELEVEN has the value 101 by E.Q. This number expresses the mystery of the first beginning; symbolising as it does the Goddess, divided for love's sake by the infinity of nothing, Zero. The division is MISERY (=101), and yet it is DIVINE (=101). With the number 101 we reach the last of the simple concepts of the nature of the archetypal Woman as described above. Where a digit has a 1 either side of it, as in 111, 121, 131, etc, it forms a glyph of two pillars divided by this number, indicating a power acting in balanced manifestation: thus 121 is balanced duality as expressed in CAPRICORN, DELICIOUS, RAPTUROUS, REJOICE, which all add up to 121.

With 131 we find *Liber AL* in balanced manifestation in words such as UNIVERSE, SUPREME, SERPENT.

141 is the balance of the four elements in the words ELEMENTS, CONTINUOUS, and BEAUTEOUS.

The number 151 represents the equilibrium of the energy of Mars with CERTAINTY, EIGHTEEN, and LIGHTENING.

161 is the Law in balanced manifestation: REMEMBER, REVERENCE, and SWEETNESSES.

There is no 171 in *Liber AL* as 7 is the root number of Our Lady of the Stars, and 7=O being the infinite zero cannot be expressed.

The number 181 is expressed in the word UNUTTERABLE and since according to *Liber AL* "eight, eighty, four hundred & eighteen" is Nothing, balanced zero cannot be borne, and hence 181 = UNUTTERABLE representing a word that cannot be spoken.

There is no single word in *Liber Al* which adds to 191. 9 is the number of Yesod: the Sphere of Illusion. Illusion cannot be in balanced manifestation: if it were it would not be illusion.

LAW adds to 6 therefore any number ending in a 6 is the law of the preceding number; for example, 16 is the law of woman (1=ONE=46=WOMAN). 16=WAR which in this case is simply the state of division that she embodies and provokes.

26 is the law of duality as in Hebrew יהוה=26, the God and Devil system.

36=MAN and SUN, the triune law of man,

the Father Son and Holy Ghost concepts which are contrasted by 46=WOMAN, the law of 4 which is the number of conservation and Jupiter, of the four seasons and four elements, all ideas tending towards the birth-life-death-afterlife cycles.

56 is the pentagram law of Isis (=56) the one beyond 4 that introduces spirit.

66 means the law(=6) is the law(=6) 66=EARTH as the manifestation of the universal law.

76 is the Goddess's law, expressed in FIVE and NINE (=76). 5=S and 9=K. These values are highly significant and much could be written about their symmetry: here it will be sufficient to remark that on the Complete Tree of Life Yesod the ninth sphere on the lower tree of Manifestation has the same value as the fifth sphere Geburah and the perfected Malkuth on the unmanifest tree of Heaven, which proves the symbol of The Fall.

86 is the infinite law and the reward of Life; it is the value of BREATH.

96=BATTLE, DESIRE, LAUGHTER, the law of the ebb and flow of illusion.

Larger numbers resume the laws but in a less archetypal manner. These numbers are static statements of what the law is, they are not actively changing things but simply the manifestation of that law. When the number 6 is followed by another number this represents the law in action, so 61 is the law of unity in action; in Hebrew this is the value of AIN or Nothing.

Numbers ending in 8 represent archetypal concepts in that they are the ground rules of one Infinity. This will be illustrated with reference to the spheres on the

Hebrew Tree of Life thereby demonstrating the way in which the E.Q. illuminates the old traditions of Western occultism. I have deliberately kept to a minimum of words remarked upon as an enormous amount could be written on this one subject, while I wish only to point out routes along which the student may travel.

18 (Kether) = GO. The mundane Chakra of Kether is named Rashith ha Gilgalim, the Primum Mobile. As Crowley said, one's only function is to go.

28 (Chocmah) = WORD, IS. In the beginning was the word and the word was with God and the word was God, to quote an old Aeon script.

38 (Binah) = JOY. This proves that the Vision of Sorrow of Binah is truly a mask for the Vision of Joy.

48 (Chesed) = DOVE, GOODLY. The DOVE was sent out from the Ark in search of land or order – Chesed. GOODLY – conforming to the Chesedic plan.

58 (Geburah) = HADIT, ORDEALS. 5 is the root number of HADIT – the smallest particle that is nowhere found, the dynamic element; the fifth Sephirah has the qualities of Justice and Severity, correcting all Karma by experiences which are seen as ORDEALS.

68 (Tiphareth) = CHANGE, PALACE. The sixth sphere is the pivot of the Tree of Life. It is the sphere of the Sacrificed God when seen from below: it is the first manifestation of Life which provokes CHANGE. Tiphareth is also the PALACE of the King.

78 (Netzach) = NUIT, FIRE. The description of the Goddess NUIT conforms to the Vision of Netzach which is of a beautiful naked woman. FIRE is the only element to have a positive title in the seventh sphere where the

7 of Wands is called Victory; its magical weapon is the Lamp, symbol of Venus.

88 (Hod) = INVOKE, MASTER. Hod is the sphere of magic.

98 (Yesod) = DELICACY, MIGHTY. The MIGHTY Foundation, the sphere of illusion with the DELICACY of the Æther of the Wise.

108 (Malkuth) = GARMENT, VISIBLE. The final manifestation in tangible or VISIBLE form, a material GARMENT ensouled with the emanations of all the other Sephiroth through Yesod.

PART FIVE

WORDS

93 IS ONE OF the key numbers in the philosophy and magick of the English Qaballa. The number will be familiar to students of Crowleyanity, both from the expression 'the 93 Current', and as the numerical value in the Greek alphabetical system of the words 'Thelema' and 'Agape', meaning 'Will' and 'Love' respectively. These correspondent ideas belong to Crowley's interpretation of the *Book of the Law* and they have nothing to do with the E.Qaballistic understanding of the numeric symbol 93.

Words in *Liber AL* that have the E.Qaballistic value 93 include BEING, DIVIDE, ENDING, TIME and UNITY, to which we may add BEGIN (an anagram of BEING). We can immediately perceive the paradoxes inherent in the number, with ideas of both beginning and ending, and uniting and dividing simultaneously presented in such a fashion as to cause logical thought to short-circuit and reason to bow, as it inevitably must, to the Infinity that is TIME=93. We know from mundane experience that Time is a most peculiar phenomenon, sometimes passing at a slow crawl, and then again vanishing with unbelievable speed, seeming to have tides and rhythms that we can only rarely tune into. Many a top-flight physicist will shudder and run away rather than converse upon the topic. 93 already looks as interesting as quicksand, and when we find that both VIRGIN and MOTHER add to 93 we know that we are going to have some trouble with this number.

The Virgin Mother is a vast archetype, and the idea of a virgin birth is a mighty powerful idea – for both the archetype and the idea reflect the Mystery of the Creation, which is happening continuously as it has always done. TIME is the VIRGIN MOTHER, bringing forth manifestation and devouring it again, uniting and dividing past and future. It seems only right therefore that NATURE too has the E.Qaballistic value 93, and thus E.Q. makes demonstrable sense of our universe from the first ripple of creation to this precise moment right now! – for in the illumination given by the correspondences of 93 we see that Mother Nature, ever Virgin, unites and divides all things in and by Time, causing things to BEGIN=93 and bringing about their ENDING=93.

We have come a long way with just nine words of the value 93. We might think of the number as being female: there is nothing straightforward about 93, but caprice and perversion are certainly present, and beauty too. Now we must extend our study beyond the realms of ideas suggested by words of significant symbolic meaning into the more practical and usefully applicable territory of Astrology; and then we will return to this curious feminine entity and discover what more we have learned about Her along the way.

93 is the value of SCORPIO, the Sign of the Scorpion. It is a Water Sign, the other two in the

Triplicity being Pisces and Cancer, and in the division of the Heavens into the twelve Houses of the Astrological chart Scorpio is assigned to the Eighth House, called the House of Death. All the Water Signs have intimations of mortality in terms of Astrological correspondences: Cancer is attributed to the Fourth House from which is discerned the end of things delineated by the chart: in the case of a nativity the Fourth House shows the circumstances of old age. The Piscean Fish is of course a Christian symbol - and the theme continues through the Hebrew letter Nun, which means a fish and is ascribed to the Death Tarot card - which brings us back once more to the Zodiac Sign attributed to the XIIIth Trump, SCORPIO=93. Given what we know so far the connection of 93 with Death does not outrage reason, and it is something of an E.Qaballistic joke that MURDER=93.

Scorpio is the Zodiacal Sign occupied by the Sun during the autumnal period from the third week of October to the third week of November. The source of the correspondence between the seasons and the Zodiac is England, the source of the language of *Liber AL*; the Signs of the Zodiac reflect the agricultural year as it is experienced in England and in Western temperate zones generally. When the Sun enters Scorpio it is already harvest time, fruit is ripened and seeds made ready. Trees seem to die as their leaves change colour and fall to the ground, where they will be transformed and incorporated into the soil. The Balance of Libra, where the Sun's entrance marks the Equinox, is now tipped into Scorpio the House of Death. It is a time of metamorphosis and mystery and apparent death; as Orion and Sirius climb into the suddenly frosty night-sky survival seems uncertain, even though close examination reveals in tiny leaf buds and bulb shoots the continuity of life and the potential promise of Spring; we instinctively light fires, and commemorate our dead in this most unsettling and peculiar of seasons.

In the divinatory branch of Astrology, called Horary Astrology, if the Moon appears between 15 degrees of Libra and 15 degrees of Scorpio then the future cannot be predicted, and the chart cannot be judged and must be discarded. Astrologers call this period the Burning Way or Via Combusta and consider it to be a dangerous portion of the heavens. In the magickal philosophy of the English Qaballa the second half of Libra and the whole Sign of Scorpio when occupied by the Moon is recognised as the time to expect the unexpected, to anticipate the unforseen, and to keep one's head down. During this time plans for the future, or seed ideas, or what you will, all undergo a period of death, during which nothing begun can possibly survive unchanged, but which sustains the mystery that is the continuity of existence. This usually involves some obstacle which arrives quite out of the blue to hamper pre-arranged activities, while undertakings and projects begun at this time are certain to develop unimaginable twists and mishaps which may lead to total ruin. These assertions are easily tested with the employment of a current ephemeris and two to three days observation of life's rich tapestry as it misses and drops a stitch.

Through the living symbol of the Zodiac and the

characteristics we have noted so far of SCORPIO(=93) revealed in the cycles of the Sun and the Moon, we can glimpse the manner in which NATURE(=93) the ever VIRGIN(=93) MOTHER(=93) goes about her Work of sustaining Life in TIME(=93). She is all TIME, expressed though the Zodiac but not bounded by it; but if one particular period may be said to be Her TIME(=93) then it is clearly SCORPIO(=93), when life appears to die or to be sacrificed or at the least undergo a sea-change, after which nothing will ever be quite the same again. Mysterious and secret and highly unlikely things happen under 93: there is some similarity with the dark of the Moon, whose deities and particular magick appear to be governed by 93.

We are now in a position to add to our earlier observations of 93 and state that the archetype symbolised by this number is extremely powerful, secretive, unpredictable, and potentially very dangerous, delighting in causing the improbable to become necessary. It touches our lives every month when the Moon passes through Libra-Scorpio. MOON+LIBRA+SCORPIO 49+58+93=200= MANIFESTATION: Moon-Libra is a still moment of Judgement before Moon-Scorpio expels us from one state to the next with all the charming yet irrevocable inevitability of a Greek tragedy. We have come to know 93 as an entity that is reliably untrustworthy, oddly humorous, and subtle as poison: and entirely necessary for the progress of the Cosmos, for She is before Creation causes the first outrageous imperfection and the division for the chance of union; it is She who makes the grit in the oyster of Eternity.

(We may remark here that COILING=93, and observe that history never repeats itself exactly, but in a coil of time there may be similar conditions or events occurring repetitively; and furthermore we suggest that Darwinian evolution can only happen by a process of 93 wherein the impossible becomes not only desirable, but essential.)

93 is represented in the physiology of the human female by the menstrual flux. The sex organs traditionally are ruled by Libra and Scorpio: the maximum fertility of the reproductive cycle is represented by the opposite Zodiacal Signs of Aries and Taurus which of course are occupied by the Sun in Springtime. Again there is the apparent death, in this case it is the womb lining that is sacrificed accompanied by the seemingly catastrophic yet not life-threatening effusion of blood, all to prepare the way for new life and the possible conception of a child. The parallel is exact, and women who know this in their hearts find their menstrual flow is anything but a tense or uncomfortable experience.

The symbolism of the Crucifixion is exactly cognate. The timing of the Christian festival of Easter Sunday is calculated according to the lunar cycle: it always follows the first full Moon after the Spring Equinox, when the Sun enters the Sign of Aries. The full Moon being opposite the Sun must of course be in Libra; and when there is a late Easter in April the Moon is full in Scorpio.

The unfolding of the mysteries of the crucifixion is a story that continues after death, and indeed it is now appropriate that we extend our investigation beyond that finality. It has been shown that certain vital forces remain attached to the body for up to 72 hours after death occurs; the stone is rolled away from the tomb after three days; and in Astro-Qaballistic terms the next Zodiac Sign is SAGITTARIUS=146=HEREAFTER, which needs no elucidation. The full story is represented in detail by the four signs Libra, Scorpio, Sagittarius, and Capricorn. Libra represents the judgement; the balance before death; the unfertilised seed in the womb. Scorpio represents the crucifixion; the onset of menstruation (BLOOD=42=CROSS); the apparent death of nature. Sagittarius represents the mysterious three days in the tomb; the period of rest following the bleed; the sleep of winter. Capricorn represents the resurrection; the renewed and restored woman; the potential for rejuvenation in Nature symbolised by the Green Man.

The cycle delineated by the four Zodiac Signs Libra, Scorpio, Sagittarius, and Capricorn is extremely significant in the English Qaballistic System. The value of LIBRA + SCORPIO + SAGITTARIUS + CAPRICORN, (58+93+146+121) in E.Q. is 418, a number which resonates throughout the *Book of the Law*. 418 is a much more precise formula than IAO, describing as it does the four stages of any endeavour from the initial planning and judgement of conditions and circumstances (LIBRA) through the inevitable set-backs and modifications (SCORPIO) to the smooth progress (SAGITTARIUS) towards achievement of the final goal (CAPRICORN). For instance, when we wish to bake a cake, we first weigh out the ingredients in the Libra stage: Scorpio sees the ingredients mixed together and losing their identity, and then all go in the oven for the Sagittarius phase where by some strange alchemy they combine into a delicious confection, to be revealed in Capricorn. Pilgrims set out full of confidence in the future and the efficacy of their arrangements; then there will be a stumbling on the way and unforseen difficulties to negotiate, and then the sheer hard toil of the journey captures the mind while the body continues on autopilot as it were, until at last the vision of the destination is transformed into tangible reality, and the journey is complete.

418 appears in the text of *Liber AL* at the end of the penultimate verse of the second chapter in the phrase "and the name of thy house 418." We know that 'house' is an Astrological term, and moreover the value of HOUSE by E.Q. is 58, a number which is also the value of ZODIAC and LIBRA. It appears that "thy house" has something to do with the four ZODIAC(=58) SIGNS(=58) mentioned above, whose sum total is 418. THY HOUSE has the value 101 which immediately suggests duality, indicating that of the four Zodiacal values in 418 the number 121 has a particular significance in this context as the most obviously dualistic of the quartet. 121 is the value of CAPRICORN the Goat whose power is derived from the three preceding Signs, and who is the Zodiacal expression of Baphomet: 418 then is the House of Baphomet, the Dual One: and the journey through the four stages delineated by Libra, Scorpio, Sagittarius, and Capricorn, is a symbol of the initiation known as THE ORDEAL X = 128 = BAPHOMET. The Ordeal X is the Ordeal of the Cross, during which all the dualities within the psyche of the candidate are balanced and effectively cancelled. THY HOUSE = 101 = ACHIEVE,

DISCOVER, DIVINE, ELEVEN and MYSTIC; these words give some idea of the transformation endured by the candidate on his way to the initiation of the House named 418; and also MISERY=101 indicating the extreme nature of the Ordeal, as part of its action is to ABROGATE=101 the upkeep of many a cherished sacred cow.

The Ordeal X is begun at the conjunction of the SUN AND VENUS = 128 =BAPHOMET and SCARLET WOMAN. Astrological synchronization, as previously stated, is an important doctrine of English Qaballistic Magick, and the Sun conjunct Venus is one of the most significant stellar configurations in the Astro-Qaballistic calendar, the positions of the aspects marking out the points of a Celestial Pentagram over a period of about eight years. In celebrating the event at the correct time we are invoking the perfection of the Pentagram into our own imperfect beings and imprinting our own microcosm onto those Five Points. The Elemental Forces become balanced within and without, in the Harmony of the Spirit. That at least is the theory, but in practice the candidate is usually so deeply flawed by fate and erroneous teachings, blocked up with useless information, and tangled in illusion, that the effect of celebrating Sun-Venus is more like a tortuous series of upheavals and explosions; for when we perform the Sun-Venus ritual we place ourselves in the hands of the metalworking gods who will melt us with fire and cool us with water and hammer us on the anvil of life until we submit to the kind of shape that the Harmony of the Spirit can actually indwell. This kind of purification takes years, possibly several lifetimes; it is an Ordeal made up of an unknown number of ordeals, cleaning house down to the bare boards and plaster as it were, as the forces we have invoked get to work in our lives and begin internally and externally altering the hitherto safe and familiar circumstances in which we have been accustomed to operate, often with disastrous consequences.

The Pentagram therefore is a most dynamic symbol of purifying, which is why the ritual known as the Lesser Banishing Pentagram Rite is so effective when properly performed. It is said that Venus contains all the planets and so we may think of Sun conjunct Venus as the Sun in conjunction with all the planets. Now in terms of magickal and Horary Astrology when a planet is conjunct the Sun it is referred to as 'combust', meaning that the Sun has consumed it and rendered it temporarily powerless; so the Sun in conjunction with Venus is a negating of all planetary influence for a moment, in which the Spirit may communicate directly with the Elements. This will result in the onset of a genuine and inescapable initiatory experience which may affect groups as well as individuals who have marked the moment with ritual, collectively or independently. In that moment we are at the Balance, just as we are when the Moon is in Libra the Sign of the Balance, ruled of course by Venus. MOON+LIBRA 49+58 = 107 = SUN+VENUS 36+71. Here we stand at the brink of Ordeal and Initiation, and our story will follow the model already described, through death in Scorpio, and into the wilderness of Sagittarius, where we will wander in darkness until the revelation of the light comes again in the dawn of Capricorn.

The most overtly dramatic period is that ruled by Scorpio. SUN+VENUS+SCORPIO 36+71+93 = 200 which as we have seen is the value of MANIFESTATION, and one of the points of the Celestial Pentagram is very often formed in Scorpio. When this particular configuration is celebrated then the processes of initiatory change is synchronised with the Sun's passage through the Zodiac. Through the 93 formula of Unity by Denial, or Division by Affirmation, the Divine Union represented by the Pentagram manifests in the microcosm of the candidate. In this rehearsal of the Ordeal X the candidate is stripped of all the ideas they have about themselves so that they are left with just two notions of what their identity is – who they are, and who they are not, or in other words, Self and Not-Self. The candidate will undergo all sorts of mental and emotional torture in this state until the sacrifice demanded by 93 is complete, and then the candidate will be reborn in the Sagittarius/ Capricorn phase as the unification of duality occurs and continues to infinity, and he becomes BAPHOMET=128 or she becomes the SCARLET WOMAN=128. 128 is the Unity (1) of Duality (2) to Infinity (8).

The E.Qaballistic philosophical attributions of the Sun-Venus Pentagram are revealed in *Liber AL* Ch.I v.53, "This shall regenerate the world," where THIS=56 means pentagrammic(5) LAW=6 or the Law of ALL=5. The Sun and Venus, Lord and Lady of the Stars, draw their Star in the Heavens and by its power the world is regenerated. SUN+VENUS=107: the 3-digit number is a composite symbol easily understood as signifying the union of being (1) and not-being (0) expressed in the

Goddess (7). MAGICIAN and SILENCE have the same value and indeed the latter is the virtue of the former. This must be so, as it is only in the Silence that Self and Not-Self can unite and thus regenerate the Magician's world. The student will be able to form his or her own personal correspondences with these ideas through the English Qaballa.

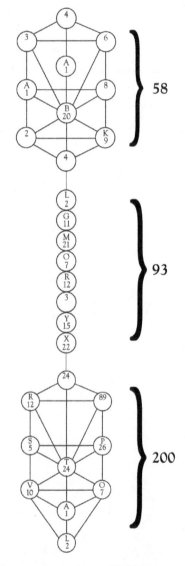

THE EXPOSITION OF LIBER AL II:76.

PART SIX

MAGICK

E.QABALLISTS USE the model of the Hebrew Tree of Life rather as an illustration of the forces at work in the manifest Universe, and in the mind of Man who exists within it as an observer. It is immaterial and beside the point to enquire as to the source of this well-known diagram: whether or not the Jews invented it, it is generally known as the Hebrew Tree and that is how I shall continue to refer to this particular design. In the English Qaballistic system however this Hebrew Tree is completed, being surmounted by a similar arrangement of ten spheres laid out in such a way as to represent the (impossible) perfection of the Hebrew Tree. This Perfect Tree is Heaven in E.Q.

This Complete Tree of Life or Two Tree System (also called the Trees of Eternity) is most often referred to as "Two Seventy-six" by the O.˙.A.˙.A.˙. because it is the solution to the sequence of numbers and letters, 28 in all, that appear in Chapter Two Verse 76 of the *Book of the Law*. (See illustration on page 73). This mystery was unlocked by Brother Leo soon after his discovery of the English Qaballa when Brother Thoth, who had a bee in his bonnet about 93 and armed with pen and calculator was engaged in tracking down every occurrence of that number in *Liber AL*, remarked that he had even found one in II:76. (Brother Thoth was a Polish magician and one of the best E.Qaballists in the O.˙.A.˙.A.˙. - he worked closely with Brother Leo in the early years and has been credited with the explanation of the Two Tree system: but he lacked the training and experience in the Hebrew Kabbalah to have solved the puzzle himself. His analytical work with E.Q. was invaluable however, and he did discover the method known as "counting well" by which the quintessence of the combination of two words may be discerned.)

The proposal of the Two Tree System is a good example of E.Qaballistic methodology. To begin with, here are two sets of ten numbers and letters united and divided by 93 = UNITY and DIVIDE. The first set adds to 58 which is the value of LIBRA, the Balance which precedes 93=SCORPIO; and HADIT which is the infinitely tiny particle, and maybe has a connection with Had "the manifestation of Nuit." (*Liber AL* Ch.1 v.1.) The last ten characters have the value of MANIFESTATION, 200, the phenomenon previously mentioned. There does appear to be a pattern emerging here, the graphemes of Chapter 2 verse 76 are not random but have some sort of relationship. So what comes in groups of ten? - the spheres on the Hebrew Tree of Life are ten in number, so do we consider two trees? Let us try the experiment. Let us draw a Hebrew Tree and put the last ten characters on it, and put the extra eight of the 93 section above Kether where the old Hebrew Kabbalists apparently ran out of ideas, and above that we will have another Tree with the remaining ten numbers and letters, this time with

Malkuth raised to the Daath centre so that it is balanced as LIBRA is balanced because these ten spheres have the value of LIBRA, and HADIT which as the infinitely tiny particle must necessarily be perfect. Now we see a truly Complete Tree with branches at the top, a trunk represented by the 93 section, and roots which have a similar form to that of the branches, whereas the trunk is of a different configuration all together. Now we see the Hebrew Tree of Life as exactly that, our life in this manifest Universe; and beyond our consciousness instead of the ill-defined Limitless Light there is the Perfect Balanced Tree of Heaven. TIME, and NATURE, both having the value 93, are what separate us from this perfection. Now too, perhaps, the "division for love's sake" becomes clearer.

Thus far, be it noted, we have not strayed beyond our understanding of *Liber AL*, except to borrow a template so old a refurbishment is overdue. But we must proceed with caution and respect. We have a composite symbol that seems to work in terms of *Liber AL*, but if there is any real truth in it there should be other reflections of that truth in other systems. Single trees are and have been sanctified with worship the world over, of course, but are there any significant examples of a pair of trees? We have a little look around and we do find stories of two Trees, in the Scandinavian Creation myth, and in the Garden of Eden, where they are called the Tree of Life and the Tree of the Knowledge of Good and Evil; and plenty of tales about lovers who are turned into trees, including the first humans after the Flood according to the Greeks. Encouraged by these distant parallels we continue to explore. Every time we think we have got something we test it against everything that we know anything about that might be relevant. Sometimes the trail peters out and we can go no further, and it may be years before we are ready to make the calculation that will clear the way before us. Other times the numbers line up like the wheels of a celestial slot machine and the pure gold of realisation cascades ecstatically into our minds, often with great humour. For the English Qaballa does have a highly developed sense of the ridiculous, and will toss out numbers in the most unlikely circumstances.

Brother Leo published an outline of the solution to II:76 in TNE/BJM Vol.6 Pt.1. Some of this article was redacted by Jake Stratton-Kent in"The Serpent Tongue"; and the Preface to the Kaaba edition of the *Book of the Law* entitled "L", contained a severely edited description of the Double Tree (as it is sometimes called) accompanied by an illustration. It may be of interest to note here that II:76 was the verse that led to the discovery of the Key to the English Qaballa. The solution to the Order and Value hidden in the grid on sheet 16 of the third day's dictation to Crowley was in fact realised a little later and published in TNE/BJM Vol.5 Pt.3, as a proof of the system rather than an account of the way in which it was unveiled.

An extended delineation of the significance of II:76 is beyond our present remit, as it is a template of infinity. Any number can be added to each of the twenty-eight spheres to decode its story from the very Highest level of Unmanifestation right down to our own Malkuth consciousness. To discover the story that brings a number to manifestation in Malkuth we simply subtract 2 from that number, and then add the result to the 28 spheres. To find how 42 (=STAR, BLOOD, CROSS etc) comes to manifestation for example, add 40 to all the spheres, and the final sum in Malkuth on the Bottom Tree will be L=2+40=42. A similar process will reveal how the highest archetypal conception of 42 comes into existence. The value of Kether in Heaven is 4 so we must add 38 to give us 42 in the Heavenly Kether, and we go on and add 38 to the values of all the other spheres down to 38+L=2=40 in the lowest sphere of Manifestation. Note that 38=JOY and 40=ALTAR.

After much experimentation with different numbers it was concluded that the addition of one of the most significant numbers in *Liber AL*, 93, yielded some of the most significant results when applied to II:76. This proposition was inspired by the use of the word "LISTEN"(=93) in the preceding verse. As occultists we must always be ready to LISTEN, and be SILENT (an anagram of LISTEN) in accordance with the Hermetic axiom "To Dare, To Know, To Will, and to Keep Silent". "Listen to the numbers & the words,"(Ch. II v.75) suggests the application of this sensory ability to the twenty-eight characters, or more simply, the addition of the value of LISTEN. Indeed, given what we have learned about 93, we may expect that the addition of this number will provide a general overview of the processes of life, death, afterlife, and rebirth. We have found that 93=TIME, the elusive domain, implacable in its measurement of our lives, in which all our experiences are formulated and remembered; and 93=NATURE in and of which we all partake, our real MOTHER(=93) from whence we came and must inevitably return in the Transformation of Death. Leo wrote in TNE/BJM Vol.6 Pt.1 that as 93 is the value of the word of the Law, Thelema, in Greek, so by adding 93 we are imposing the word of the Law upon the NUMBERS & THE WORDS = MANIFESTATION. In fact the addition of 93 to the spheres of the Complete Tree of Life is in itself proof unassailable of the validity of the symbol.

With the addition of 93 we find that both Kether and Yesod on the Tree of Heaven have the value 97 which is the value of NOTHING, and the reward of 79=HEAVEN. This correspondence resonates with *Liber AL* III:1, "Abrahadabra! The reward of Ra Hoor Khut," where ABRAHADABRA=79 and RA HOOR KHUT=97. 97 is also the value of PISCES, the last Sign of the Zodiac which traditionally is held to contain all the other Zodiac Signs. In terms of the English Qaballa, then, Heaven begins and ends in a concept of Nothing which contains all things. The Heavenly Tiphareth has the value 113 = I AM LIFE ("and the Giver of Life," *Liber AL* Ch.II v.6), and CENTRE, and SPIRIT; demonstrating with great and subtle simplicity that the Kingdom of Heaven has at its very heart the principle of LIFE=68=JESUS.

The enumeration of the Bottom Tree with 93 confirms the Creation Myth as it is given in the first chapter of *Liber AL*. We quote the relevant section in full for the sake of clarity later on:

"None, breathed the light, faint & faery, of the stars, and two. For I am divided for love's sake, for the chance of union. This is the creation of the world, that the pain of division is as nothing, and the joy of dissolution all." (*Liber AL* I: 28-30).

Both BREATHED and THE LIGHT have the value 117. This is the number of Kether in manifestation, 24+93=117. We may associate "breathed" with the Breath of Life which is the same after a different fashion as the primordial Light of Kether. 117 is also the value of GEMINI the Twins or the Brothers: this correspondence is referring to the Duality of the Division for Love's Sake, and encompasses the more traditional view of Kether whose Sacred Countenance is ever half hidden. Oddly enough, Crowley in his Book of Thoth states that Atu VI, the Tarot Trump to which Gemini is assigned "in its original form, it was the story of Creation." *Liber AL* gives a Name for this number, HOOR PAAR KRAAT=117, of whom Aiwass is the Minister, (*Liber AL* I:7). MYSTERY=117 so we may read the verse as "None, breathed Mystery (or Hoor Paar Kraat), faint & faery, of the stars..."

The use of the word NONE is of course quite deliberate; it has the same value as DEATH, 60, where we might prefer it to be 97=NOTHING, which has almost the same meaning in English as "none" and since neither Brother Leo nor Jake Stratton-Kent saw fit to explain further neither will we, except to point out that Death is an intrinsic necessity of Life, and thus the value of the word adds to the picture of active duality. In his article published in TNE/BJM Vol.6 Pt.1 Leo proposed that NONE as Zero is parallel to "Ain Soph" and therefore the next word should indicate Kether, which as *Liber AL* I:28 shows, is the case with the word BREATHED = THE LIGHT.

The apparent duality of Kether is reflected again in Tiphareth where T=24+93=117; naturally, because "no man cometh unto the Father but by me," (KJV, John 14:6). The value of Malkuth in Manifestation is L=2+93=95. Here 93 resolves the dualities of L=2 in 95 = THE STAR (53+42), THE CROSS, THE SIN, etc. Note that 2 is in the Mercurial sphere of Hod on the Tree of Heaven, and L=2 is the first symbol of the 93 section which continues with G=11 (1 and 1), M=21 (2 and 1). The Double Tree is permeated with balanced dualities or divisions for love's sake. THE LIGHT is both FAINT & FAERY = 151 = LIBRA + SCORPIO: again the pairing of symbols is harmonious as it must be because the division is for love's sake.

The Scorpio formula of Unity by Denial is the formula of the Goddess who is divided for love's sake, both UNITY and DIVIDE having the value 93. Other words in *Liber AL* adding to 93 are NATURE and TIME and BEING, indicating that the conditions and patterns of life on earth conform exactly to the original pattern of creation as symbolised by the Two Trees where 93 unites and divides the upper and lower Trees. Lees wrote that "Meditation upon the Two Trees makes all the systems of the psyche work in integrated harmony, because there is a wholeness into which all the energies of the spirit may pour with no leakage of force into spurious negative existence, where it can be allowed to breed monsters of gods who need no justification for their actions. All powers on the completed Tree of Life justify their actions by being part of the whole cycle of life as reflected here on earth in the fertility cycle of woman, and in the cycles of the Moon, Sun, and Stars. This Tree is the blueprint upon which any system in human experience, past, present, and future, can be explained in terms of natural phenomena."

In *Liber AL* I:30 we find the words "PAIN OF DIVISION" = 200 = MANIFESTATION. This is all Manifestation, and it is all subject to the Pain of Division; we need not illustrate this phenomenon further, although we may note here that DISSOLUTION has the same value as SACRIFICE, 133

Love is the only factor that can unite the divided. This principle is especially relevant to understanding the words "Do what thou wilt shall be the whole of the Law" and the completion of the statement with "Love is the Law, Love under Will." This means that every action of the will must be for love's sake, for the chance of union. Thus the spiritual basis of the English Qaballa and the *Book of the Law* is the same as any other true doctrine of spirituality, in that it advocates Love as the one force supreme in and of Creation.

We should also note that *Liber AL* II:76 is the 142nd verse in the *Book of the Law*. Now there is no single word in *Liber AL* that adds up to 142 by English Qaballa, and it is the first number in the sequence from 10 to 231 to have no single word attributed to it. The number 142 has a variety of significant correspondences. It is a resonance of "None...and Two" where NONE=60=DEATH whose traditional number is 14, the value of N which as Nun in Hebrew is ascribed to the Death Card, the 14th Tarot

Trump; and 2 is TWO, the Woman of the Star of Whom we do not speak. 142 is the first three decimal places of pi, and it is shorthand for the 14th February, Valentine's Day, when women traditionally choose their mate. 142 is not quite within this plane of existence, for it partakes closely in the Mysteries of the Goddess and the Magick of Creation. Thus MOON + SCORPIO = 142, Scorpio being the House of Death, as described elsewhere.

The Moon is closely associated with II:76 since there are 28 spheres on the Complete Tree, and 28 days in the lunar cycle. 28 is the value of WORD: II:76 is itself a Word beyond articulation. This clarifies the old tradition that women cannot rise above a certain Grade, being unable to pronounce the Word of a Magickian – but by her very nature ruled as it is most intimately by the Moon, Woman embodies the Word which she cannot utter.

One last remark is appropriate. If we add 2 to the spheres of the Bottom Tree then its sum total becomes 220. This allows us to ascribe the 220 verses of the *Book of the Law* to the Ten Sephiroth, an exercise which is well worth the effort.

AFTERWORD

IT IS NO COINCIDENCE that *Liber AL* contains words
which are of peculiar significance to all sorts of spiritual
disciplines and magickal paradigms: and be they Voodoo
or Hindu or Jewish or Heathen or Buddhist or Gnostic
or Freemasonic or Christian or Islamic or Rosicrucian or
Pagan, the English Qaballa is the Universal Solvent that
fuses them all together into one living expression of the
Present here-and-now. It affirms the notion of a single
global civilisation, broken by cataclysm, splintered and
scattered across Time into innumerable systems; some
of whose remnants are now lost altogether while some
are only just discernible in weathered stone and artificial
landscape and scraps of parchment, others surviving
doggedly on, more or less intact and determined yet
confused: a jigsaw with pieces missing or defaced almost
beyond recognition. English Qaballa cleans up the
fragments and puts them all back together again, gently
teaching us that everything is connected to everything
else and nothing happens in isolation. Civilisations
come and go but there is that which remains always.
The white brilliance above the head is the same white
brilliance as ever it was, name it how you will, symbolise
it as seems best: Baphomet's torch is the Sun-disk and

the Thousand-petalled Lotus and the Halo and the First Swirlings and the Light Higher than Eyesight. The Cross in the Circle is everybody's cross-in-the-circle, whether it be in last year's cornfield or in the ancient oriental crown of a sculptured deity, or at a roadside or at a grave, or consecrated in stone and glazed tile and stained glass. Through the English Qaballa we can contact the archetypes as they exist in our own time for us to see with our own eyes and invoke in our own language, without twisting our minds and our tongues about in the attempt to do this as it was once done hundreds or thousands of years ago. We are in the New Aeon, or the New Age, and so it is nothing less than appropriate that we have a new Book and a new Magickal language. The realities haven't changed one iota, but humanity is an evolutionary species and our spiritual consciousness evolves also; the *Book of the Law* and the English Qaballa indicate the next evolutionary initiation through which unites the divided under the glory of the stars – for love's sake – each for himself.

APPENDIX I

1. A
5. AH ALL HA
6. AS LAW
7. O
9. WAS
10. KA
11. HAD HO OH
12. LOW SAD SO
13. ADD DO RA
14. HOW SHALL WHO
15. ALSO AN NA OLD
16. WAR
17. HAWK
18. CALL GO RA'S
19. AF ASAR HOLD OR SHOW WAY
20. ASKS AWAY GLAD
21. AND NO ON SAY
22. AM DAY HAWK'S US WHY X
23. CALLS FALL HARD I SLAY
24. CLAWS DOG GLASS GOD NOW ODDS OWN WAND
    WAYS
25. AT HALF HAND LOOK OF TA
26. GOLD SAYS SON WHOSO

27. ALWAYS DAYS ILL LORD PA

28. ANKH CAN COLD DARK HOLY IS WE WOODS WORD

29. DOGS GODS HE ISA OX SKY

30. ANY DOWN DRAG FLOW HAIL HANDS HOOR KHU
   NAY WANGA WILL WORLD

31. CRAWL GOOD NU PALL SHADOWS SOUL TO WORK

32. DOOR HIS KAABA LAID LAST LORDS LOUD OIL WELL
   WHAT

33. ALOUD FOLD HATH HELL KNOW NOR RAYS SEAL
   SWORD WAST WORDS

34. DEAL DEW FOOL HAST LONG SHE TWO

35. BY FLY HANGS LAUGH [NON] SAID WHOM

36. AMN DRAWN FOLK GOODS HEAD KILL MAN MASK
   MY OUR SHALT SOULS SUN SWOON TALK

37. ART AVAIL DUSK FOR IN MAY PASS ROYAL SONG
   SWELL

38. AIWASS ARE DEAD DWELL HARM HELL'S JOY NIA
   ONLY SWORDS TOO WEAK

39. ARMS AUM AWAKE FOLLOW FOOLS FULL KHABS
   LOSE TASK YOU

40. ALTAR CRY GROSS HAIR HARDLY HAVE HOST HOUR
   LURK PAAR SAKE SHED WOES YE

41. AWFUL AYE DOTH HER IF SAVE WEAR WHOLE YEA

42. BLOOD CROSS DAMN DOST HEAR KISS NEW SIN
   SKEW STAR WANT

43. BACK BOOK BRASS CAST DIN DOES EACH FOODS
   JOYS LIARS OFF RED RUN SLAVE THAN THY UP
   WORM

44. DARE FAIL FOLLY LOVE PLAY WHOSE WRATH

45. BE BLACK END FILL NOT SLAIN

46. EASY FEW FLOOR INK KIN ME ONE SORROW SWEAR

TOY WHEN WOMAN

47. BOND BROWS COWARDS EGG FELL FLAP FOAM
    GLORY IT KNOWN KRAAT SHOOT STARS USE
    WHICH WRONG

48. BODY CHILD DOVE DUNG GOODLY HIM LUST
    MARKS OUT SLAVES

49. ALONE BID CALLED CROWN JEWS KEY LIT LOVE'S
    MARY MEAL MOON RISK ROSE SOLVE

50. AGAIN AXLE BES COPH DREAD EAT FADE HARLOT
    LIE RAIN RARE SELF SEND SHOWED SIX STAND
    THUS

51. ADORE BED CARE DRUGS ISLAND KNEW KRAATH
    LARGE LET MANY ONES SINK SORROWS SORRY TRY
    YOUR

52. AEONS BUY CLOSE DONE DUST ITS NIGH POOR
    PUSH RICH THOU WET WILT

53. CAKES CLEAR DRESS LAZULI MADE ORDEAL SIGN
    SING TELL THAT THE

54. AMONG BIG DIE FLESH FOUR GUMS HATE KHUT
    LEARN MISS OVER PALE SET SNAKE SOFT VAULT
    WITH

55. BLISS BOTH CATCH EAST MUCH NAKED SEAT SEE
    STANDS VALUE WANDED

56. BEDS CHANT [FACT] FEAR KHONSU LEST LOVER
    MAKE NECH RULE SHROUDS STILL THIS WINGS
    WISE YOURS

57. AROUND AUGHT CANST CORE ELSE FACE HELP
    HURT KING LAPIS MOST OBEAH SAITH TOP TORN
    WEST WHILE

58. ABASED BARE BEAR COLOUR DROOP DRUNK FROM
    HADIT HERU HIDE HOUSE ORDEALS SIGNS SOME

SPARKS SWEAT
59. GRAVE KIBLAH LIKE ONCE READY REWARD TAKE
WHEEL
60. AHATHOOR ARDOURS BOSOM COWER DEATH DENY
EVIL GET GLEAM GRADES HARDER LIVE MEN NONE
SPELL VEIL VITAL
61. AMEN ARCHED BUT CARESS CHOOSE CLERK COPY
FIND HONOUR LOVELY NAME RULES SHAPE
62. ALREADY ANIMAL BOWELS FALLEN FELLOWS FOUND
HOPE JUST KINGS LOCKED MASSES MONGOL
ORDER POUR SACRED TEAR TUM UNTO
63. ABOVE ADORER AZURE BIND BURN LEAVE MAUT
64. BEHOLD BLUE BOUND DIDST DRINK FRESH
LANGUOR LIGHT LINE PAIN REASON ROBE SEEK
STIR TWIN UPON WEAVE WHEELS YET
65. ADORANT ASSUAGE BEND BLIND FORTH GLOBE
HONEY LIVES LYING MORE PEN RISE SPELLS THOSE
WATER WERE WINE WISDOM
66. ARGUE ARISE BABE CALLING CHARGE COME DIRE
EARTH FOOLISH GATES HEART HERE LOFTY MEANS
MIX RAISE REST SPEAK
67. AROUSE FLAME HEADED JOYOUS LIFT MASKED MUST
OBEY OLIVE PLACE PUT SIGHT SKIES STAIN STOPS
STUDY TEACH THEN THOUGH THRILL TURN YEARN
68. BURNS CHANGE CHOSEN DINE INTO JESUS LIDDED
LIFE ORISON PALACE PROUD RAPID SMOOTH THEY
69. ABOUT DANGER DYING GIVE GLADNESS LEFT
SAYING SEEN SPARE STARRY THIRD WHERE WIFE
70. ABSOLVE ARMOUR BEAT BENDS CHANCE EYES
FAITH FEEL GIRT KNOWER PROOF SECOND SPACE
TRULY WARRIOR WOMEN

71. AGELONG FAERY GLOBED HEARTS LIMBS LONGER
    PILLARS STYLE SURPASS VICE
72. ATTACK CHASTE CURSE EVER FLOWERS KISSES
    OPEN OTHER TOMB
73. CANNOT CONSOLE DAMNED DEMAND FATES FEAST
    FORGE GREAT GROUP HOLIER KEEN PECK PIT
    POWER RA-HOOR-KHU RUNES STORE STRONG
    SWIFT TAKEN THICK
74. ASSUME BEST DISCUSS DOUBT EVEN EXALT GIVES
    RIGHT SENSE SPEARS THEM THINK UNDER
75. ABIDE ARIGHT BEAST CITY COUNT CUBE FACTOR
    FORCE MANYHOOD REVEAL SYMBOLS   UNION
    WARRIORS
76. COILED FIVE HERU-RA-HA JEWELS NIGHT NINE SEEM
    THING VICES WITHDRAW
77. CURSES DEEM DEVOUR DOUBLE ENJOY GATHER
    KHUIT NOUGHT OTHERS SERVE SILVER STAMP
    VENOM
78. CRIES ENOUGH FEASTS FIRE HIDDEN LITHE
    MANTRAS NUIT SPIT TEST THEE TRUE UNKNOWN
    WILLING
79. ABRAHADABRA AGAINST CONSOLED HEAVEN
    HIGHER HOMEWARD RITUAL STATE THROUGH
    WORKING YONDER
80. AFTER BAHLASTI BEASTS BEGGAR BRING FAINT
    FIGHT FINE LENGTH PURE SINCE SINGLE STONES
    UNTIL VIGOUR WORSHIP
81. APPEAL GIVER HIDING IMAGE INDIAN KHEPHRA
    KNOWING LOVE-SONG PASTE STEEL STELE TA-NECH
    THINGS TRUTH
82. BALANCED CRUSHED DEEP FIRST FOURTH LONGING

MONEY SCARLET SWEET WINGED

83. CHIEF DISSOLVE GIVEN MERE MIDDLE MIGHT MINE
SEETH SHRINE SUCCESS THESE

84. BEEN CONVEY ENGLISH GLORIOUS HAWK-HEADED
HUNDRED KEPT NAMING RITUALS WHENCE

85. CONSOLER JASPER MAKEST NEMYSS REIGN RESULT
SHUNNED SOLDIERS SQUARED VISIT

86. BEWARE BREATH BRIDE COURAGE CREEDS FILTHY
FORBID IMAGES KNOWETH LOATHING MERCY
NEVER SCENTS THRONE

87. ANOTHER ARMIES BEYOND BREAST BURNT EIGHT
EVERY FIFTH FOURFOLD GREEN KINSFOLK
KNOWEST MONTHLY VERILY WEAKNESS WRITE

88. BLESSED BREED CIRCLE ECSTASY FULLNESS INVOKE
LIKEST MASTER MODEST NATIONS PERIL PITY
SHEETS THEBAN THEIR

89. [ATOMIC] CATTLE HEADDRESS OBTAIN SIXTY
SPANGLES TRANCE

90. APOSTLE AVAILETH FEVER FLAMING KISSING
NOWHERE OMPEHDA PAPER PEACE SUDDENLY
SUNSET THERE THINE THREE TRIED UNLIKE

91. ANSWERED APPEAR AVAILEST EAGERLY FOREST
FORSAKEN HERSELF LEAVINGS OUTCAST RIGHTLY
SERVANT SIGHING SPRING STAR-LIT TREES VEILED
[WHITER] WITHIN

92. ACCURSED CARESSED FEET HITHER MILLION
MOCKERS PRIDE READING STRANGE UNDERGO

93. APPAREL BEING COILING DIVIDE ENDING LISTEN
ORDERED ORIGINAL POURED SHAMELESS SOFTEN
TAHUTI THYSELF TIME UNITY

94. BRIGHT COMETH DEPART DESTROY GIRDERS SISTER

TRODDEN WHEREOF
95. DELIGHT PERISH SELF-SLAIN SYSTEM
96. BATTLE CONFOUND DESIRE HIGHEST LAUGHTER
    MINGLE REMAIN SERVANTS UNFIT UNVEILS
    WINNERS
97. BATHING COMPANY DESERT GIVETH GREET
    HEATHEN ITSELF NOTHING PURGED RA-HOOR-
    KHUT READETH SECURE SPHERE SPICES
98. CLUSTER COVERED DELICACY EATING EXHAUST
    FAILURE FIFTY HIMSELF LIFTED MIGHTY QUICKLY
    SCRIBE SKEW-WISE SMITE STRIKE TIMES TONGUE
    WHOSOEVER
99. CHILDREN DIVIDED INDEED SORROWETH STRIVE
100. ADORATIONS CRAPULOUS DAUGHTER DEADLIER
    ENTER HRUMACHIS LITTLE LOVE-CHANT
    QUEEN
101. ABROGATE ACHIEVE DESIRES DISCOVER DIVINE
    ELEVEN MENTU MISERY MYSTIC REMAINS
102. AFTERWARD BEAUTY BEGONE CONSUME EIGHTY
    ENTRAP KNOWLEDGE LEAPING REFUSE
    SEVERE UNASSUAGED WITHOUT
103. ALPHABET BOTTOM DIREFUL DISPOSED ETERNAL
    FRIENDS LIGHTEN SEEING SMELLING SPEAKER
    STANDETH THEBES TONGUES UNITE
104. DECIDED HOOR-PA-KRAAT MYSTICAL OVERTHROW
    SECRET VICTORY WONDERFUL
105. BLESSING BUDDHIST CONVERT HURTING JASMINE
    KNEWEST NIGHT=SKY OBJECT
106. ANYTHING BECAUSE CONCEALED DISREGARDS
    MOHAMMED REVEALED STARLIGHT
107. BEAUTY'S BEFORE CONQUER LAMBENT MAGICIAN

MATTER SILENCE TROUBLE

108. FORTRESS GARMENT MISTAKE PURPLE REFUGE RESINOUS SPELLING STATURE TRAITORS VEILING VISIBLE

109. BROTHERS ESTABLISH GEMMED HERMIT MEANING NUMBER OVERMUCH OVERSEE REGRET STRANGELY

110. GREATER POWERFUL QUARTER STRONGER WRITING

111. BECOME BREATHE BURNING DIVISION EMPTY INVOKING PEOPLE THEREON TRAMPLE

112. CERTAIN ENGINE FURTHER LETTER WRETCHED

113. BENDING CENTRE GARMENTS PLEASURE PRINCE SERVICE TOUCHING

114. BLINDNESS BUSINESS DESOLATION FORTIES HERMITS HUNGERED MEANETH NUMBERS REDEEM SPLENDOUR TRANSLATED

115. ALIENATE DESPISE MEANEST NINETY PRIEST QUARTERS SHRINKING THEREOF UNIQUE VIRTUOUS WRITINGS

116. ADULTEROUS EXCEED FIERCE PEOPLES WRITEST

117. BREATHED BURNEST DEFUNCT EXPOUND FORTIFY HOOR-PAAR-KRAAT LETTERS MYSTERY RAPTURE REFINE STOOPING SUPPORT

118. ALL-TOUCHING ANKH-AF-NA-KHONSU CENTRES MIRACULOUS PRINCES PURPOSE SPACE-MARKS

119. ABRAMELIN BLASPHEMY CLERK-HOUSE CREATION DESIRABLE EMBLEMS EMPRESS INCENSE MOREOVER POVERTY PROMISE SPLENDROUS STRENGTH SWEETER UTTERLY

120. ESPECIAL ILL-ORDERED OVERCOME RA-HOOR-

KHUIT RA-HOOR-KHU-IT STREETS

121. DELICIOUS DESPISED MOUNTAIN RAPTUROUS
REJOICE TORTURE

122. COMPASSION

123. EARNESTLY NIGHT-STARS PINNACLES REVEALING
TEMPLE THREEFOLD UNDERSTOOD

124. CONQUEST [NON-ATOMIC] PROMISES PROPHET
UNDERSTAND

125. ARGUMENT COMMENT DISAPPEAR DROPPING
POINTED THEREBY WRITTEN

126. BEETLES CONQUEROR CONTENTS MIDNIGHT
PARTICLE SHATTERED

127. EQUINOX NEITHER THEREIN THROUGHOUT
TORMENT UNTOUCHED

128. BES-NA-MAUT PRECIOUS RIGHTEOUS WAR-ENGINE
WICKEDNESS

129. AN-HUNGERED EXHAUSTED INVIOLATE POSITION
PROPHETS TREMBLE

130. BETTER EQUATION MULTIPLY PRINTED SPECTRE

131. AZURE-LIDDED ENTHRONED EXORCIST FORBIDDEN
PASSIONATE PROTECT SERPENT SUPREME
UNIVERSE

132. BLUE-LIDDED DOUBLE-WANDED EYESIGHT
SUBTLETY SUFFERER VOLUPTUOUS

133. DISSOLUTION FOURSQUARE LAUGHTERFUL
PERCHANCE SACRIFICE UNDESIRED

134. DELIVERED INSPIRED UNATTACKED

135. BRILLIANCE EXPECT SIXTY-ONE

136. BETWEEN HERU-PA-KRAATH

137. ULTIMATE WORSHIPPED

138. ENEMIES VENGEANCE

139. ENGINERY EXPOSURE JUDGMENTS QUESTIONS UNVEILING
140. EIGHTIES HIEROPHANT NIGHT-BLUE
141. BEAUTEOUS CONTINUOUS ELEMENTS UPLIFTED VICTORIOUS
143. MIGHTIER PERFECT TERRIBLE WORSHIPPER
144. PERFUME REJOICING
145. INNERMOST INVISIBLE PRESENCE PROFESSIONAL
146. CONCUBINE DRUNKENNESS HEREAFTER
147. BEAUTIFUL EXTENDED MINISTER
148. INNOCENCE MEETINGS PRESENTLY WORSHIPPERS
149. CREEPING MEETEST PERFUMES
150. PRIESTESS
151. CERTAINTY EIGHTEEN LIGHTENING
152. EXCELLENT INTELLECT PERFORMED THEREFORE
153. CONSCIOUSNESS
154. THEREUPON
155. ABOMINATION INTIMATE MYSTERIES TENDERNESS
156. EVERYWHERE STAR-SPLENDOUR
157. EMPHATICALLY
158. CENTURIES
159. UTTERMOST
160. ABSTRUCTION
161. REMEMBER REVERENCE SWEETNESSES
162. ETERNITY
164. BEAUTIFULLY INFINITE
165. PENETRANT
166. EXPECTED
167. TRIBULATION [UN(F)RAGMENTARY]
168. FORTH-SPEAKER
170. ATTRIBUTE

APPENDIX II

A=1
ABASED=58
ABIDE=75
ABOMINATION=155
ABOUT=69
ABOVE=63
ABRAHADABRA=79
ABRAMELIN=119
ABROGATE=101
ABSOLVE=70
ABSTRUCTION=160
ACCURSED=92
ACHIEVE=101
ADD=13
ADORANT=65
ADORATIONS=100
ADORE=51
ADORER=63
ADULTEROUS=116
AEONS=52
AF=19
AFTER=80
AFTERWARD=102

AGAIN=50
AGAINST=79
AGELONG=71
AH=5
AHATHOOR=60
AIWASS=38
ALIENATE=115
ALL=5
ALL-TOUCHING=118
ALONE=49
ALOUD=33
ALPHABET=103
ALREADY=62
ALSO=15
ALTAR=40
ALWAYS=27
AM=22
AMEN=61
AMN=36
AMONG=54
AN=15
AND=21
AN-HUNGERED=129
ANIMAL=62
ANKH=28
ANKH-AF-NA-KHONSU=118
ANOTHER=87
ANSWERED=91
ANY=30
ANYTHING=108
APOSTLE=90

APPAREL=93
APPEAL=81
APPEAR=91
ARCHED=61
ARDOURS=60
ARE=38
ARGUE=66
ARGUMENT=125
ARIGHT=75
ARISE=66
ARMIES=87
ARMOUR=70
ARMS=39
AROUND=57
AROUSE=67
ART=37
AS=6
ASAR=19
ASKS=20
ASSUAGE=65
ASSUME=74
AT=25
[ATOMIC=89]
ATTACK=72
ATTRIBUTE=170
AUGHT=57
AUM=39
AVAIL=37
AVAILEST=91
AVAILETH=90
AWAKE=39

AWAY=20
AWFUL=41
AXLE=50
AYE=41
AZURE=63
AZURE-LIDDED=131

BABE=66
BACK=43
BAHLASTI=80
BALANCED=82
BARE=58
BATHING=97
BATTLE=96
BE=45
BEAR=58
BEAST=75
BEASTS=80
BEAT=70
BEAUTEOUS=141
BEAUTIFUL=147
BEAUTIFULLY=164
BEAUTY=102
BEAUTY'S=107
BECAUSE=106
BECOME=111
BED=51
BEDS=56
BEEN=84
BEETLES=126

BEFORE=107
BEGGAR=80
BEGONE=102
BEHOLD=64
BEING=93
BEND=65
BENDING=113
BENDS=70
BES=50
BES-NA-MAUT=128
BEST=74
BETTER=130
BETWEEN=136
BEWARE=86
BEYOND=87
BID=49
BIG=54
BIND=63
BLACK=45
BLASPHEMY=119
BLESSED=88
BLESSING=105
BLIND=65
BLINDNESS=114
BLISS=55
BLOOD=42
BLUE=64
BLUE-LIDDED=132
BODY=48
BOOK=43
BOND=47

BOSOM=60
BOTH=55
BOTTOM=103
BOUND=64
BOWELS=62
BRASS=43
BREAST=87
BREATH=86
BREATHE=111
BREATHED=117
BREED=88
BRIDE=86
BRIGHT=94
BRILLIANCE=135
BRING=80
BROTHERS=109
BROWS=47
BUDDHIST=105
BURN=63
BURNEST=117
BURNING=111
BURNS=68
BURNT=87
BUSINESS=114
BUT=61
BUY=52
BY=35

CAKES=53
CALL=18

CALLED=49
CALLING=66
CALLS=23
CAN=28
CANNOT=73
CANST=57
CARE=51
CARESS=61
CARESSED=92
CAST=43
CATCH=55
CATTLE=89
CENTRE=113
CENTRES=118
CENTURIES=158
CERTAIN=112
CERTAINTY=151
CHANCE=70
CHANGE=88
CHANT=56
CHARGE=66
CHASTE=72
CHIEF=83
CHILD=48
CHILDREN=99
CHOOSE=61
CHOSEN=68
CIRCLE=88
CIRCUMFERENCE=231
CITY=75
CLAWS=24

CLEAR=53
CLERK=61
CLERK-HOUSE=119
CLOSE=52
CLUSTER=98
COILED=76
COILING=93
COLD=28
COLOUR=58
COME=66
COMETH=94
COMMENT=125
COMPANY=97
COMPASSION=122
COMPLEMENT=178
CONCEALED=106
CONCUBINE=146
CONFOUND=96
CONQUER=107
CONQUEROR=126
CONQUEST=124
CONSCIOUSNESS=153
CONSOLE=73
CONSOLED=79
CONSOLER=85
CONSUME=102
CONTENTS=126
CONTINUITY=174
CONTINUOUS=141
CONVERT=105
CONVEY=84

COPH=50
COPY=61
CORE=57
COUNT=75
COURAGE=86
COVERED=98
COWARDS=47
COWER=60
CRAPULOUS=100
CRAWL=31
CREATION=119
CREEDS=86
CREEPING=148
CRIES=78
CROSS=42
CROWN=49
CRUSHED=82
CRY=40
CUBE=75
CURSE=72
CURSES=77

DAMN=42
DAMNED=73
DANGER=69
DARE=44
DARK=28
DAUGHTER=100
DAY=22
DAYS=27

DEAD=38
DEADLIER=100
DEAL=34
DEATH=60
DECIDED=104
DEEM=77
DEEP=82
DEFUNCT=117
DELICACY=98
DELICIOUS=121
DELIGHT=95
DELIVERED=134
DEMAND=73
DENY=60
DEPART=94
DESERT=97
DESIRABLE=119
DESIRE=96
DESIRES=101
DESOLATION=114
DESPISE=115
DESPISED=121
DESTROY=94
DEVOUR=77
DEW=34
DIDST=64
DIE=54
DIFFERENCE=179
DIN=43
DINE=68
DIRE=66

DIREFUL=103
DISAPPEAR=125
DISCOVER=101
DISCUSS=74
DISPOSED=103
DISREGARDS=106
DISSOLUTION=133
DISSOLVE=83
DIVIDE=93
DIVIDED=99
DIVINE=101
DIVISION=111
DO=13
DOES=43
DOG=24
DOGS=29
DONE=52
DOOR=32
DOST=42
DOTH=41
DOUBLE=77
DOUBLE-WANDED=132
DOUBT=74
DOVE=48
DOWN=30
DRAG=30
DRAWN=36
DREAD=50
DRESS=53
DRINK=64
DROOP=58

DROPPING=125
DRUGS=51
DRUNK=58
DRUNKENNESS=146
DUNG=48
DUSK=37
DUST=52
DWELL=38
DYING=69

EACH=43
EAGERLY=91
EARNESTLY=123
EARTH=66
EAST=55
EASY=46
EAT=50
EATING=98
ECSTASY=88
EGG=47
EIGHT=87
EIGHTEEEN=151
EIGHTIES=140
EIGHTY=102
ELEMENTS=141
ELEVEN=101
ELSE=57
EMBLEMS=119
EMPHATICALLY=157
EMPRESS=119

EMPTY=111
END=45
ENDING=93
ENEMIES=138
ENGINE=112
ENGINERY=139
ENGLISH=84
ENJOY=77
ENOUGH=78
ENTER=100
ENTHRONED=131
ENTRAP=102
EQUATION=130
EQUINOX=127
ESPECIAL=120
ESTABLISH=109
ETERNAL=103
ETERNITY=162
EVEN=74
EVER=72
EVERY=87
EVERYWHERE=156
EVIL=60
EXALT=74
EXCEED=116
EXCELLENT=152
EXHAUST=98
EXHAUSTED=129
EXISTENCE=178
EXORCIST=131
EXPECT=135

EXPECTED=166
EXPIRATION=177
EXPOSURE=139
EXPOUND=117
EXTENDED=147
EYES=70
EYESIGHT=132

FACE=57
[FACT=56]
FACTOR=75
FADE=50
FAERY=71
FAIL=44
FAILURE=98
FAINT=80
FAITH=70
FALL=23
FALLEN=62
FATES=73
FEAR=56
FEAST=73
FEASTS=78
FEEL=70
FEET=92
FELL=47
FELLOWS=62
FEVER=90
FEW=46
FIERCE=116

FIFTY=98
FIFTH=87
FIGHT=80
FILL=45
FILTHY=86
FIND=61
FINE=80
FIRE=78
FIRST=82
FIVE=76
FLAME=67
FLAMING=90
FLAP=47
FLESH=54
FLOOR=46
FLOW=30
FLOWERS=72
FLY=35
FOAM=47
FOLD=33
FOLK=36
FOLLOW=39
FOLLY=44
FOODS=43
FOOL=34
FOOLISH=66
FOOLS=39
FOR=37
FORBID=86
FORBIDDEN=131
FORCE=75

FOREST=91
FORGE=73
FORSAKEN=91
FORTH=65
FORTH-SPEAKER=168
FORTIES=114
FORTIFY=117
FORTRESS=108
FOUND=62
FOUR=54
FOURFOLD=87
FOURSQUARE=133
FOURTH=82
FRESH=64
FRIENDS=103
FROM=58
FULL=39
FULLNESS=88
FURTHER=112

GARMENT=108
GARMENTS=113
GATES=66
GATHER=77
GEMMED=109
GET=60
GIRDERS=94
GIRT=70
GIVE=69
GIVEN=83

GIVER=81
GIVES=74
GIVETH=97
GLAD=20
GLADNESS=69
GLASS=24
GLEAM=60
GLOBE=65
GLOBED=71
GLORIOUS=84
GLORY=47
GO=18
GOD=24
GODS=29
GOLD=26
GOOD=31
GOODLY=48
GOODS=36
GRADES=60
GRAVE=59
GREAT=73
GREATER=110
GREEN=87
GREET=97
GROSS=40
GROUP=73
GUMS=54

HA=5
HAD=11

HADIT=58
HAIL=30
HAIR=40
HALF=25
HAND=25
HANDS=30
HANGS=35
HARD=23
HARDER=60
HARDLY=40
HARLOT=50
HARM=38
HAST=34
HATE=54
HATH=33
HAVE=40
HAWK=17
HAWK-HEADED=84
HAWK'S=22
HE=29
HEAD=36
HEADDRESS=89
HEADED=67
HEAR=42
HEART=66
HEARTS=71
HEATHEN=97
HEAVEN=79
HELL=33
HELL'S=38
HELP=57

HER=41
HERE=66
HEREAFTER=146
HERMIT=109
HERMITS=114
HERSELF=91
HERU=58
HERU-PA-KRAATH=136
HERU-RA-HA=76
HIDDEN=78
HIDE=58
HIDING=81
HIEROPHANT=140
HIEROPHANTIC=176
HIGHER=79
HIGHEST=96
HIM=48
HIMSELF=98
HIS=32
HITHER=92
HO=11
HOLD=19
HOLIER=73
HOLY=28
HOMEWARD=79
HONEY=65
HONOUR=61
HOOR=30
HOOR-PAAR-KRAAT=117
HOOR-PA-KRAAT=104
HOPE=62

HOST=40
HOUR=40
HOUSE=58
HOW=14
HRUMACHIS=100
HUNDRED=84
HUNGERED=114
HURT=57
HURTING=105

I=23
IF=41
ILL=27
ILL-ORDERED=120
IMAGE=81
IMAGES=86
IN=37
INCENSE=119
INDEED=99
INDIAN=81
INFINITE=164
INITIATING=180
INK=46
INNERMOST=145
INNOCENCE=148
INSPIRATION=172
INSPIRED=134
INTELLECT=152
INTIMATE=155
INTO=68

INVIOLATE=129
INVISIBLE=145
INVOKE=88
INVOKING=111
IS=28
ISA=29
ISLAND=51
IT=47
ITS=52
ITSELF=97

JASMINE=105
JASPER=85
JESUS=68
JEWELS=76
JEWS=49
JOY=38
JOYOUS=67
JOYS=43
JUDGMENTS=139
JUST=62

KA=10
KAABA=32
KEEN=73
KEPT=84
KEY=49
KHABS=39
KHEPHRA=81

KHONSU=56
KHU=30
KHUIT=77
KHUT=54
KIBLAH=59
KILL=36
KIN=46
KING=57
KINGS=62
KINSFOLK=87
KISS=42
KISSES=72
KISING=90
KNEW=51
KNEWEST=105
KNOW=33
KNOWER=70
KNOWEST=87
KNOWETH=86
KNOWING=81
KNOWLEDGE=102
KNOWN=47
KRAAT=47
KRAATH=51

LAID=32
LAMBENT=107
LANGUOR=64
LAPIS=57
LARGE=51

LAST=32
LAUGH=35
LAUGHTER=96
LAUGHTERFUL=133
LAW=6
LAZULI=53
LEAPING=102
LEARN=54
LEAVE=63
LEAVINGS=91
LEFT=69
LENGTH=80
LEST=56
LET=51
LETTER=112
LETTERS=117
LIDDED=68
LIARS=43
LIE=50
LIFE=68
LIFT=67
LIFTED=98
LIGHT=64
LIGHTEN=103
LIGHTENING=151
LIKE=59
LIKEST=88
LIMBS=71
LINE=64
LISTEN=93
LIT=49

LITHE=78
LITTLE=100
LIVE=60
LIVES=65
LOATHING=86
LOCKED=62
LOFTY=66
LONG=34
LONGER=71
LONGING=82
LOOK=25
LORD=27
LORDS=32
LOSE=39
LOUD=32
LOVE=44
LOVE-CHANT=100
LOVELY=61
LOVER=56
LOVE'S=49
LOVE-SONG=81
LOW=12
LURK=40
LUST=48
LYING=65

MADE=53
MAGICIAN=107
MAGNIFICENT=187
MAKE=56

MAKEST=85
MAN=36
MANIFESTATION=200
MANTRAS=78
MANY=51
MANYHOOD=75
MARKS=48
MARY=49
MASK=36
MASKED=67
MASSES=62
MASTER=88
MATTER=107
MAUT=63
MAY=37
ME=46
MEAL=49
MEANEST=115
MEANETH=114
MEANING=109
MEANS=66
MEETEST=149
MEETINGS=148
MEN=60
MENTU=101
MERCY=86
MERE=83
MIDDLE=83
MIDNIGHT=126
MIGHT=83
MIGHTIER=143

MIGHTY=98
MILLION=92
MINE=83
MINGLE=96
MINISTER=147
MIRACULOUS=118
MISERY=101
MISS=54
MISTAKE=108
MIX=66
MOCKERS=92
MODEST=88
MOHAMMED=106
MONEY=82
MONGOL=62
MONTHLY=87
MOON=49
MORE=65
MOREOVER=119
MOST=57
MOUNTAIN=121
MUCH=55
MULTIPLY=130
MUST=67
MY=36
MYSTERIES=155
MYSTERY=117
MYSTIC=101
MYSTICAL=104

NA=15
NAKED=55
NAME=61
NAMING=84
NATIONS=88
NAY=30
NECH=56
NEITHER=127
NEMYSS=85
NEVER=86
NEW=42
NIA=38
NIGH=52
NIGHT=76
NIGHT-BLUE=140
NIGHT-SKY=105
NIGHT-STARS=123
NINE=76
NINETY=115
NO=21
[NON=35]
[NON-ATOMIC=124]
NONE=60
NOR=33
NOT=45
NOTHING=97
NOUGHT=77
NOW=24
NOWHERE=90
NU=31
NUIT=78

NUMBER=109
NUMBERS=114

O=7
OBEAH=57
OBEY=67
OBJECT=105
OBTAIN=89
ODDS=24
OF=25
OFF=43
OH=11
OIL=32
OLD=15
OLIVE=67
OMNIPRESENCE=210
OMPEHDA=90
ON=21
ONCE=59
ONE=46
ONES=51
ONLY=38
OPEN=72
OR=19
ORDEAL=53
ORDEALS=58
ORDER=62
ORDERED=93
ORIGINAL=93
ORISON=68

OTHER=72
OTHERS=77
OUR=36
OUT=48
OUTCAST=91
OVER=54
OVERCOME=120
OVERMUCH=109
OVERSEE=109
OVERTHROW=104
OWN=24
OX=29

PA=27
PAAR=40
PAIN=64
PALACE=68
PALE=54
PALL=31
PAPER=90
PARTICLE=126
PASS=37
PASSIONATE=131
PASTE=81
PEACE=90
PECK=73
PEN=65
PENETRANT=165
PEOPLE=111
PEOPLES=116

PERCHANCE=133
PERFECT=143
PERFORMED=152
PERFUME=144
PERFUMES=149
PERIL=88
PERISH=95
PESTILENCE=182
PILLARS=71
PINNACLES=123
PIT=73
PITY=88
PLACE=67
PLAY=44
PLEASURE=113
POINTED=125
POOR=52
POSITION=129
POUR=62
POURED=93
POVERTY=119
POWER=73
POWERFUL=110
PRECIOUS=128
PRESENCE=145
PRESENTLY=148
PRIDE=92
PRIEST=115
PRIESTESS=150
PRINCE=113
PRINCE-PRIEST=228

PRINCES=118
PRINTED=130
PROFESSIONAL=145
PROMISE=119
PROMISES=124
PROOF=70
PROPHET=124
PROPHETS=129
PROTECT=131
PROUD=68
PURE=80
PURGED=97
PURPLE=108
PURPOSE=118
PUSH=52
PUT=57

QUARTER=110
QUARTERS=115
QUEEN=100
QUESTIONS=139
QUICKLY=98

RA=13
RA-HOOR-KHU=73
RA-HOOR-KHUIT=120
RA-HOOR-KHU-IT=120
RA-HOOR-KHUT=97
RAIN=50

RAISE=66
RAPID=68
RAPTURE=117
RAPTUROUS=121
RARE=50
RA'S=18
RAYS=33
READETH=97
READING=92
READY=59
REASON=64
RED=43
REDEEM=114
REFINE=117
REFUGE=108
REFUSE=102
REGENERATE=174
REGRET=109
REIGN=85
REJOICE=121
REJOICING=144
REMAIN=96
REMAINS=101
REMEMBER=161
REPRODUCTION=186
RESINOUS=108
REST=66
RESTRICTION=182
RESULT=85
REVEAL=75
REVEALED=108

REVEALING=123
REVERENCE=161
REWARD=59
RICH=52
RISE=65
RIGHT=74
RIGHTEOUS=128
RIGHTLY=91
RISK=49
RITUAL=79
RITUALS=84
ROBE=64
ROSE=49
ROYAL=37
RULE=56
RULES=61
RUN=43
RUNES=73

SACRED=62
SACRIFICE=133
SAD=12
SAID=35
SAITH=57
SAKE=40
SAVE=41
SAY=21
SAYING=69
SAYS=26
SCARLET=82

SCENTS=86
SCRIBE=98
SEAL=33
SEAT=55
SECOND=70
SECRET=104
SECURE=97
SEE=55
SEEING=103
SEEK=64
SEEM=76
SEEN=69
SEETH=83
SELF=50
SELF-SLAIN=95
SEND=50
SENSE=74
SERPENT=131
SERVANT=91
SERVANTS=96
SERVE=77
SERVICE=113
SET=54
SEVERE=102
SHADOWS=31
SHALL=14
SHALT=36
SHAMELESS=93
SHAPE=61
SHATTERED=126
SHE=34

SHED=40
SHEETS=88
SHOOT=47
SHOW=19
SHOWED=50
SHRINE=83
SHRINKING=115
SHROUDS=56
SHUNNED=85
SIGHING=91
SIGHT=67
SIGN=53
SIGNS=58
SILENCE=107
SILVER=77
SIN=42
SINCE=80
SING=53
SINGLE=80
SINK=51
SISTER=94
SIX=50
SIXTY=89
SIXTY-ONE=135
SKEW=42
SKEW-WISE=98
SKIES=67
SKY=29
SLAIN=45
SLAVE=43
SLAVES=48

SLAY=23
SMELLING=103
SMITE=98
SMOOTH=68
SNAKE=54
SO=12
SOFT=54
SOFTEN=93
SOLDIERS=85
SOLVE=49
SOME=58
SON=26
SONG=37
SORROW=46
SORROWETH=99
SORROWS=51
SORRY=51
SOUL=31
SOULS=36
SPACE=70
SPACE-MARKS=118
SPANGLES=89
SPARE=69
SPARKS=58
SPEAK=66
SPEAKER=103
SPEARS=74
SPECTRE=130
SPELL=60
SPELLING=108
SPELLS=65

SPHERE=97
SPICES=97
SPIT=78
SPLENDOUR=114
SPLENDROUS=119
SPRING=91
SQUARED=85
STAIN=67
STAMP=77
STAND=50
STANDETH=103
STANDS=55
STAR=42
STARLIGHT=106
STAR-LIT=91
STARRY=69
STARS=47
STAR-SPLENDOUR=156
STATE=79
STATURE=108
STEEL=81
STELE=81
STILL=56
STIR=64
STONES=80
STOOPING=117
STOPS=67
STORE=73
STRANGE=92
STRANGELY=109
STREETS=120

STRENGTH=119
STRIKE=98
STRIVE=99
STRONG=73
STRONGER=110
STUDY=67
STYLE=71
SUBTLETY=132
SUCCESS=83
SUDDENLY=90
SUFFERER=132
SUN=36
SUNSET=90
SUPPORT=117
SURPASS=71
SUPREME=131
SWEAR=46
SWEAT=58
SWEET=82
SWEETER=119
SWEETNESSES=161
SWEET-SMELLING=185
SWELL=37
SWIFT=73
SWOON=36
SWORD=33
SWORDS=38
SYMBOLS=75
SYSTEM=95

TA=25
TAHUTI=93
TAKE=59
TAKEN=73
TALK=36
TA-NECH=81
TASK=39
TEACH=67
TEAR=62
TELL=53
TEMPLE=123
TENDERNESS=155
TERRIBLE=143
TEST=78
THAN=43
THAT=53
THE=53
THEBAN=88
THEBES=103
THEE=78
THEIR=88
THELEMITES=178
THEM=74
THEN=67
THERE=90
THEREBY=125
THEREFORE=152
THEREIN=127
THEREOF=115
THEREON=111
THEREUPON=154

THESE=83
THEY=68
THICK=73
THINE=90
THING=76
THINGS=81
THINK=74
THIRD=69
THIS=56
THOSE=65
THOU=52
THOUGH=67
THREE=90
THREEFOLD=123
THRILL=67
THRONE=86
THROUGH=79
THROUGHOUT=127
THUS=50
THY=43
THYSELF=93
TIME=93
TIMES=98
TO=31
TOMB=72
TONGUE=98
TONGUES=103
TOO=38
TOP=57
TORMENT=127
TORN=57

TORTURE=121
TOUCHING=113
TOY=46
TRAITORS=108
TRAMPLE=111
TRANCE=89
TRANSLATED=114
TREES=91
TREMBLE=129
TRIBULATION=167
TRIED=90
TRODDEN=94
TROUBLE=107
TRUE=78
TRULY=70
TRUTH=81
TRY=51
TUM=62
TURN=67
TWIN=64
TWO=34

ULTIMATE=137
UNASSUAGED=102
UNATTACKED=134
UNDER=74
UNDERGO=92
UNDERSTAND=124
UNDERSTANDETH=177
UNDERSTOOD=123

UNDESIRED=133
UNFIT=96
[UN(F)RAGMENTARY=167]
UNIMAGINABLE=172
UNION=75
UNIQUE=115
UNITE=103
UNITY=93
[UNIVERSALITY=171]
UNIVERSE=131
UNKNOWN=78
UNLIKE=90
[UNMOLESTABILITY=223]
UNTIL=80
UNTO=62
UNTOUCHED=127
UNUTTERABLE=181
UNVEILING=139
UNVEILS=96
UP=43
UPLIFTED=141
UPON=64
US=22
USE=47
UTTERLY=119
UTTERMOST=159

VALUE=55
VAULT=54
VEIL=60

VEILED=91
VEILING=108
VENGEANCE=138
VENOM=77
VERILY=87
VICE=71
VICES=76
VICTORIOUS=141
VICTORY=104
VIGOUR=80
VIRTUOUS=115
VISIBLE=108
VISIT=85
VITAL=60
VOLUPTUOUS=132

WAND=24
WANDED=55
WANGA=30
WANT=42
WAR=16
WAR-ENGINE=128
WARRIOR=70
WARRIORS=75
WAS=9
WAST=33
WATER=65
WAY=19
WAYS=24
WE=28

WEAK=38
WEAKNESS=87
WEAR=41
WEAVE=64
WELL=32
WERE=65
WEST=57
WET=52
WHAT=32
WHEEL=59
WHEELS=64
WHEN=46
WHENCE=84
WHERE=69
WHEREOF=94
WHICH=47
WHILE=57
[WHITER=91]
WHO=14
WHOLE=41
WHOM=35
WHOSE=44
WHOSO=26
WHOSOEVER=98
WHY=22
WIFE=69
WICKEDNESS=128
WILL=30
WILLING=78
WILT=52
WINE=65

WINES=70
WINGS=56
WINGED=82
WINNERS=96
WISDOM=65
WISE=56
WITH=54
WITHDRAW=76
WITHIN=91
WITHOUT=102
WOES=40
WOMAN=46
WOMEN=70
WONDERFUL=104
WOODS=28
WORD=28
WORDS=33
WORK=31
WORKING=79
WORLD=30
WORM=43
WORSHIP=80
WORSHIPPED=137
WORSHIPPER=143
WORSHIPPERS=149
WRATH=44
WRETCHED=112
WRITE=87
WRITEST=116
WRITING=110
WRITINGS=115

WRITTEN=125
WRONG=47

X=22

YE=40
YEA=41
YEARN=67
YET=64
YONDER=79
YOU=39
YOUR=51
YOURS=56

APPENDIX III

SUN=36
MOON=49
MERCURY=115
VENUS=71
MARS=39
JUPITER=143
SATURN=73
URANUS=66
NEPTUNE=145
PLUTO=76

ARIES=66
TAURUS=76
GEMINI=117
CANCER=78
LEO=34
VIRGO=63
LIBRA=58
SCORPIO=93
SAGITTARIUS=146
CAPRICORN=121
AQUARIUS=95
PISCES=97